What people are saying about *Writing to Win Federal Grants...*

Cassidy and Kester have captured the very essence of government grant development and presented it in a format useful to both the novice and seasoned writer. Their helpful hints, checklists, and progressive descriptions bring clarity and logic to a process that challenges even the best professionals. This is truly the step-by-step guide we've all been waiting for!

Lisa M. Chutjian, CFRE

Chief Development Officer, Alexander Graham Bell Association for the Deaf and Hard of Hearing; National Chair, Grant Professionals Foundation

What a great resource for folks seeking federal grants... I wish that I had read such a book before I started on my current employment of working with many federal agencies. This is an excellent guide to working with federal agencies in general. There is a wealth of useful tips that can help a grant seeker immediately, plus lessons for the long term.

Richard Redfearn, PhD

Grant Programs Manager, Sam M. Walton College of Business, University of Arkansas

This is one of the best books on government grants I have seen. It puts the complicated task of developing, writing, and submitting a federal grant into a logical, straightforward, and easy-to-understand approach.

Tracey Diefenbach

Director of Grants, Big Brothers Big Sisters of Eastern Missouri

Writing to Win Federal Grants *is the best insider's guide to a successful federal grants program. The chapters on logical frameworks, budgets and budget narratives, and project and evaluation plans are especially helpful. A grants professional who can get these items up to par for federal grants can take on any proposal or project development challenge! I plan to have my entire foundation team read this and to give copies to my colleagues in HR, finance, and senior leadership... because the information in this book is so applicable to every grants office!*

Heather Lane

Senior Director of Institutional Giving, Oceana: Protecting the World's Oceans

The grant process can be overwhelming sometimes, so the authors' pep talks are helpful, while the insider tips, examples, and stories from the real world helped me focus on important topics. The checklists and worksheets will be very useful. In fact, I am using your chapter on evaluation as I'm working on my NSF proposal. Overall, a great product and a great guide to proposal writing!

Robert M. Block, PhD

Associate Dean of Engineering and Applied Science, University of Colorado Colorado Springs

Writing to Win Federal Grants *is an amazing resource for an organization looking to learn the ins and outs of grant writing. I am confident in saying this book will lead you to the bright future of federal grant awards. Chapter Six will get you through the toughest of times!*

Camille Brown

Grants Office Coordinator, Ozarks Medical Center Grant Development

Writing to Win Federal Grants *provides a deep dive into the process of writing a federal grant without making the reader feel bogged down or overwhelmed. The workbook provides incredibly helpful tools, several of which I will likely "steal." These two books will be great contributions to our body of knowledge.*

Teri Blandon
Vice President, Institutional Advancement, Global Communities

In the grants industry, it's rare to find resources devoted to federal grant seeking, especially ones that are relevant across multiple sectors. For municipalities pursuing government funding, this book is a must-have! *This book has become a remarkable asset and resource to my staff. In fact, I plan on purchasing a copy for my entire staff and for many of our clients too. The authors' strong and clear writing style is complemented well by their advanced technical knowledge and industry expertise.*

Tia Cavender, GPC
President, Chase Park Grants

Writing to Win Federal Grants *is not only a comprehensive manual for the grants professional who is just beginning to tackle the complexity of federal grants, but it will be a wonderful resource for experienced veterans! Written in a simple, easily understandable conversational style,* **Writing to Win Federal Grants** *also makes a wonderful textbook and resource for those of us who teach grant writing courses at colleges and universities. If I had* **Writing to Win Federal Grants** *when I first began preparing and writing federal grants, it would have saved me an enormous amount of time and helped prevent some embarrassing faux pas!*

Kent Hornberger, GPC
Principal, Gateway Grant Solutions

Even after fifteen years in this profession, I found **Writing to Win Federal Grants** *chock-full of helpful advice and new ways to understand federal grants. This book contains the most understandable explanation of the use of the logic model I've ever read!*

Barb Putman
Executive Director, Community Creative Center

Finally, a resource that not only outlines the process but also guides you, at your pace, to greater understanding and should lead to more Notice of Grant Awards! **Writing to Win Federal Grants** *is the new standard resource for learning the ins and outs of the federal grant seeking process. If you want a comprehensive, easy-to-understand resource to take your federal grant seeking to the next level of success, you want,* **Writing to Win Federal Grants**.

Emerson M. Goodwin
Corporate Regional Director, KentuckyCare

Writing to Win Federal Grants

A Must-Have for Your Fundraising Toolbox

Cheryl L. Kester, CFRE
Karen L. Cassidy, GPC

Writing to Win Federal Grants:
A Must-Have for Your Fundraising Toolbox

One of the **In the Trenches**™ series

Published by
CharityChannel Press, an imprint of CharityChannel LLC
424 Church Street, Suite 2000
Nashville, TN 37219 USA

CharityChannel.com

ISBN Print Book: 978-1-938077-61-6 | ISBN eBook: 978-1-938077-62-3

Library of Congress Control Number: 2014951121

13 12 11 10 9 8 7 6 5 4 3 2 1

Printed in the United States of America

This and most CharityChannel Press books are available at special quantity discounts for bulk purchases for sales promotions, premiums, fundraising, or educational use. For information, contact CharityChannel Press, 424 Church Street, Suite 2000, Nashville, TN 37219 USA. +1 949-589-5938

Publisher's Acknowledgments

This book was produced by a team dedicated to excellence; please send your feedback to editors@charitychannel.com.

We first wish to acknowledge the tens of thousands of peers who call charitychannel.com their online professional home. Your enthusiastic support for the **In the Trenches**™ series is the wind in our sails.

Members of the team who produced this book include:

Editors

Acquisitions Editor: Linda Lysakowski

Comprehensive Editor: Melanie Palmer

Copy Editor: Jill McLain

Production

In the Trenches Series Design: Deborah Perdue

Layout Editor: Jill McLain

Administrative

CharityChannel LLC: Stephen Nill, CEO

Marketing and Public Relations: John Millen

About the Authors

Cheryl L. Kester

Cheryl L. Kester is a Certified Fundraising Executive (CFRE). As owner of The Kester Group, she provides grant seeking and grant evaluation services for a range of clients nationwide. With almost thirty years of experience in the nonprofit sector, Cheryl has extensive expertise serving academic, faith-based, public safety, health care, and social service organizations. She has helped secure more than $96 million in state, federal, and foundation grants and contracts. An engaging speaker, Cheryl teaches grants classes, presents at conferences, and conducts board workshops. She also serves as a grant reviewer for private and federal funders. She is a member of the Association of Fundraising Professionals (AFP), the Council for the Advancement and Support of Education (CASE), and the Grant Professionals Association (GPA). In 2012, Cheryl received the GPA president's award for service to the grants profession and the association.

Cheryl's proposals have secured funds from several state and federal departments and agencies:

- Arkansas Biomedical Research Infrastructure Network (NIH sub-awards)
- Arkansas Department of Health
- Arkansas Workforce Investment Board
- Colorado Department of Public Health and Environment
- Department of Agriculture (USDA)
- Department of Education (National Professional Development, TRIO programs [Student Support Services, Upward Bound], Title III, Title V, Title VI [International Studies and Foreign Language])

- Department of Health and Human Services (ACF, CDC, and HRSA)
- Department of Homeland Security (FEMA)
- Department of Labor
- Department of State
- Environmental Protection Agency
- National Endowment for the Arts
- National Science Foundation
- West Virginia Department of Education

Karen L. Cassidy

Karen L. Cassidy, GPC and Principal of Governmental Grants Professionals LLC, began her career in the US House of Representatives working for Congressmen Bob Wise and Dick Gephardt. Transitioning into the nonprofit field, Karen applied her knowledge to help educational institutions and nonprofit organizations obtain and manage more than $250 million in grant awards. With nearly twenty-five years of experience, Karen helps organizations design programs and evaluation strategies, develop grant proposals, and report outcomes. She is presently serving as an evaluator on several foundation and federal grants.

A knowledgeable and energetic trainer, Karen leads workshops and teaches seminars on many topics, including federal grant proposal development at conferences, universities, and community nonprofits. Her experience developing successful proposals led her to become a reviewer for federal and private funders, providing her with unique insight.

Karen is one of the founding members of the St. Louis Regional Chapter, Grant Professionals Association (GPA). In October 2011, she was elected to serve on the national GPA board of directors. She earned her GPC (Grant Professional Certification) credential from the Grant Professionals Certification Institute in 2011.

Karen's proposals have secured grants from several departments and agencies:

- Corporation for National and Community Service
- Department of Commerce
- Department of Education (Office of Innovation and Improvement, FIPSE, Title V, Upward Bound, Veterans Upward Bound, and Title III)
- Department of Health and Human Services (ACF, ACYF, CDC, HRSA, NIH, and SAMHSA)
- Department of Homeland Security
- Department of Housing and Urban Development
- Department of Labor
- Department of State
- Department of Treasury
- Department of Veterans Affairs
- Environmental Protection Agency
- National Endowment for the Humanities
- National Science Foundation
- Small Business Administration
- USAID

Dedication

Karen dedicates this book to her husband and son, who put up with the crazy deadlines and demands for iced tea, Coca-Cola, and other cravings. All the chocolate chip cookies in the world can never repay either for their support and patience.

Cheryl wishes to dedicate this book to her late husband, who always supported her dreams. He may have been surprised that this book actually got done, but he would have been proud.

Authors' Acknowledgments

We wish to thank all of our clients and colleagues who were willing to share grants stories and excerpts from their grant proposals. We have learned so much from you and are grateful for your support.

- ARcare, Augusta, Arkansas

- Bridges to Wellness, Siloam Springs, Arkansas

- John Brown University, Siloam Springs, Arkansas

- Pima County Community College, Tucson, Arizona

- Lessie Bates Davis Neighborhood House, East St. Louis, Illinois

- Ozarks Medical Center, West Plains, Missouri

- Lutheran Senior Services, St. Louis, Missouri

Special thanks to the following:

- Camille Brown, Grant Development, Ozarks Medical Center

- Jerry Burka, Real Estate Consultant, Old Orchard Consulting Inc.

- Christopher Coleman, Lessie Bates Davis Neighborhood House

- Kent Hornberger, Principal, Gateway Grant Solutions

- Melanie Palmer, Executive Director of the Northwest Arkansas Women's Shelter

- Diego Uriburu, Executive Director of Identity, Gaithersburg, Maryland

Contents

Summary of Chapters

How Federal Grants Work. Understanding how reviewers score applications
and how funding agencies make their decisions about who should receive
grants will help you submit proposals that are more competitive. In this chapter,
we also introduce you to important terms and address the issue of faith-based
organizations competing for federal funds.

Are We Ready for Federal Grants? Before you even ask if you are ready to write
government proposals, you need to know whether your organization can deliver
a grant-funded program and has the capacity to meet the grant's reporting
requirements. We help you assess your grant readiness and give you concrete steps
to take to prepare to apply.

Building Your Grants Dream Team. It takes a village to pull together a grant
proposal. We explain the essential contributions various people can make to your
grant application. We follow up with tips for avoiding some of the pitfalls of working
in groups.

Finding the Best Match: Prospect Research. We recommend proactive research
strategies so you are informed as far in advance as possible of upcoming grant
opportunities. You can do the searching yourself for free, and we explain how to
build your prospect list through a combination of proven strategies.

Deciding When to Go for It: Assessing an RFA. Follow along with us on a step-
by-step introduction to the highlights of federal grant guidelines. A prioritized
list will help you make a quick, well-informed go or no-go decision about each
grant opportunity.

Mapping Out Your Journey: Logic Models. Based on the key elements of program planning, logic models help reviewers understand your program by giving a snapshot of your major program activities and their impact. We give you a fill-in-the-box method of building logic models and let you practice your skills with a fun project.

Budgets and Budget Narratives. Yes, we talk about the budget before you even begin writing your narrative. This is because the budget drives your project. Our budget checklist will help you make sure nothing essential gets left out. We also tell you how to avoid expensive mistakes when budgeting for personnel. Real-life examples show you how to craft clear, persuasive budget narratives.

Tackling the Blank Page: How to Start Writing. Once you have decided to apply for a particular opportunity, it's time to dig in to the guidelines. The evaluation criteria provide an excellent start as a writing outline. We also share insider tips about writing style, with several excerpts from grant proposals and RFAs provided as examples.

Proposal Sections: Need. A persuasive need section builds up the reviewers' expectations for the solution—your program. Need sections for government proposals are usually more about data than heart-warming stories, so we tell you how to find and use that data.

Proposal Sections: Project Description. Your description of your project has to be specific and thorough enough that reviewers are convinced you've planned it thoroughly, without drowning them in details. We show you how to balance narrative descriptions with tables to break up the text and communicate complicated processes. We also explain timelines and work plans, with samples of each to give you models to work from.

Proposal Sections: Goals and Objectives. Your project's goals and objectives set the stage for defining success. We give a clear explanation of the difference between process objectives and outcome objectives, along with advice about how to set performance targets for your objectives.

Proposal Sections: Organizational Capacity and Quality. Any time you get the chance to talk about how experienced, responsible, and successful your organization is, jump on it. Different agencies use different information to determine if they should trust their grant funds to your organization, such as your financial practices, your processes for making sure grants stay on track, and your capacity to handle the grant project.

Chapter Thirteen 125
Proposal Sections: Evaluation Plan. Evaluation plans can be intimidating—until you recognize you can break them down into predictable parts. We give you the information you need to keep your evaluation plan focused on outcomes and linked back to your project objectives. We talk about how to work with an external evaluator to make both your jobs easier.

Chapter Fourteen 137
Until Grant Do Us Part? Partnerships and Collaborations. Collaborating with other community organizations is important and sometimes required. We give you practical tips and steps to develop community collaborations, including advice on how to create a good Memorandum of Understanding (MOU).

Chapter Fifteen 145
Submitting Your Application. After you've written all of the parts of the narrative, you still aren't finished. We give you advice about putting the finishing touches on your narrative so it's ready to submit. Then we tackle the most common forms and attachments you will be asked to include in your applications. Finally, we invite you to click "submit."

Chapter Sixteen 155
After the Award: Grants Management Tips. Congratulations on winning your grant! We give you some important follow-up steps to take when you get a funding decision. These will help you run your grant more smoothly and make receiving another grant more likely. We also show you how being proactive at the beginning of the project makes your life much easier when it's time to send required reports to the funding agency.

Foreword

"Plan your work for today and every day, then work your plan." — Margaret Thatcher

Cheryl Kester and Karen Cassidy are two grant professionals with a combined thirty-five years of experience and nearly $350 million in grants approved from a variety of funding sources, local and private, who collaborated to write *Writing to Win Federal Grants*. This book is truly a must-have for the new and experienced grant writer and one that should be in the grant writer's collection as a resource of not only grant writing tools but fundraising tools as well.

In sixteen inspiring, motivating, and engaging chapters, the reader receives practical and in-depth discussions—from determining your organization's readiness to apply for federal grants to finding the appropriate funding agency to writing the narrative to reviewing the final checkpoints of what happens once the grant is approved.

Chapters One through Five are focused on prewriting activities—assessing readiness to compete, developing the dream team, finding the funding opportunity best for your organization, and assessing the RFA. Chapters Six through Thirteen provide a step-by-step or tutorial of writing the narrative. Particularly of importance here is that the authors recommend developing a logic model in Chapter Six that can serve as the big-picture view of your proposed program model. Of course, you can go back and modify it later. This is a very interesting approach because they recommend "beginning with the end in mind" as a mechanism of what you hope to achieve, which allows the reviewer to see your overall program design from a wholistic perspective. Chapter Fourteen discusses the importance of partnerships and collaborations and why MOUs are important tools for program implementation, ensuring that two or more organizations can play successfully in the sandbox. Chapter Fifteen discusses finalization and submission of the grant application, while Chapter Sixteen discusses the importance of the grant writer's continued involvement once the grant is funded. I totally agree with this since the grant writer has the big picture and probably is the person who most fully understands all the integral components of the funded application.

The authors guide you through a step-by-step process like they are your personal grant writing coaches, using humor as an effective way to keep you engaged in the grant writing process. Throughout the book, I am reminded of two principles I teach and follow when writing grants: *Follow The Guidelines* (FTG) and *Make A Case For Support* (MACFS). They accomplish this by providing sidebars with practical tips, definitions, stories from the real world, important points, and food for thought. The reader should pay particular attention to this invaluable information. The authors also mention a workbook that is available as a complement to the book—with additional practical information, including samples of logic models, budget templates, a budget narrative, a reviewer's scoring matrix, work plans, etc.

This reader/learner-friendly book begins with an overview of each chapter and ends with a recap of the important points covered. This technique reinforces the discussion of each chapter so you will be able to understand the important points before moving to the next chapter. As an experienced grant writer and trainer, I found myself receiving confirmation of what I have done throughout my years of facilitating grant writing workshops, writing grants to a variety of funders, and being a federal grant reviewer over the past twenty-plus years. Confirmation is a good thing!

Another important aspect of this book is that the authors provide insightful viewpoints from the reviewer's perspective so that grant writers can use these practical tips to strengthen their grant applications. Also, the importance of communicating with program officers is stressed.

The book concludes with an appendix section that includes thirteen additional resource materials for the grant writer. Included is a glossary of terms, list of federal funding agencies with website addresses, federal grant reviewer opportunities, and various checklists (organization information, funding opportunity feasibility, budget plans), along with recommended reading and training opportunities.

Finally, I applaud my colleagues for including the Grant Professionals Association Code of Ethics as Appendix M, which illustrates the grant profession field's commitment to ethical behavior, which can be considered one of our core values.

Thanks to Cheryl and Karen for this invaluable must-have fundraising toolbox resource.

Bernard Turner, EdD, GPC
Associate Professor of Social Entrepreneurship, Belmont University
Board Member, Grant Professionals Association

Introduction

Maybe you are a new grant professional who wants to learn more about federal grants and how to pursue them. Perhaps you are an experienced grant professional wanting to expand your organization's grant funding base. Maybe you are wondering if federal grants are right for your organization. Or perhaps you've wanted to pursue federal grants, but their complexity was a little intimidating.

Even if you are none of these people—but you need to write a federal grant proposal—this book is for you.

Several chapters of this book are devoted to the major elements of most federal grant proposals (need, project design, evaluation plan, and so on). Before jumping in, though, we familiarize you with the grants process and help you make an honest assessment of your organization's resources and its capacity to purse and manage a federal grant.

We then follow up with chapters on the budget, the attachments, how to bring in collaborators, and an overview of managing the grant after you receive it.

The most important aspect of this book is that we don't just tell you how to write a compelling need statement or evaluation plan. We show you. Excerpts from actual proposals demonstrate the advice we give you in the text.

We have you covered from start to finish.

What to Expect from This Book

This book is written by two authors who have been writing and winning federal grants for more than thirty-six years. We have been staff members at nonprofits large and small. We had to learn to work within (or help create) organizational cultures to support federal grant seeking. Now, as external consultants with our own firms, we assist clients nationwide with their federal grant seeking and grant evaluations.

We wrote this book from "in the trenches." Really. We were juggling book writing duties with federal proposals that needed to get out the door. In fact, we switched back and forth from proposals to the book, adding more real-life tips or new chapter sections as we went along.

Because of that, you get the "real-world" perspective, not an idealization of how trouble-free grant writing should work. We sometimes offer you a model of how something should be if it were ideal, but we will also tell you how it usually works in real life, with tips to make your life a little easier.

Because this is a book from the **In the Trenches** series, you can expect an accessible writing style that doesn't bury you in lots of jargon and super long sentences. At least we define the jargon when we *do* let it creep in. We do our best to help you wade through the alphabet soup of federal acronyms.

Finally, we are pleased to announce that *Writing to Win Federal Grants* is accompanied by a companion workbook. *Writing to Win Federal Grants–The Workbook* allows us to provide longer examples from actual proposals and includes many other resources, such as checklists and planning tools, that we use in our work. Throughout this text, we will let you know when more information about a topic is available in the workbook. Because the two texts are being released together, they stand independent of one another but also support each other extremely well.

Assumptions Made

We assume that you have some familiarity with the grants profession and the world of nonprofits. We do define terms such as "goals," "RFAs," and "budget," but we do not spend a lot of time on the very basics. There are several fine books that provide an introduction to grant writing.

While this book is titled *Writing to Win Federal Grants*, the principles in this book are just as applicable to winning state or local funds, whether those are grants, loans, or contracts.

We also assume that you either work for or are a consultant to an eligible grant-seeking organization. In addition to nonprofits, this may include some for-profit entities or governmental agencies, such as state governments, tribal governments, municipalities, or economic development corporations.

When speaking of applicants, we use the term "organization" to encompass higher education, health care, research, social services, the arts, and government entities. It is a convenient shorthand that saves us (and you) from having to suffer through this list of every possible eligible applicant every time we talk about applicants. When speaking of the government entities that award grants, we refer to them as "agencies." In this book, agencies are funders, and organizations are applicants.

This book includes several excerpts from actual proposals written by the authors. Text in excerpts follows the format and personal style of each proposal's author. While the two of us clearly have different styles in some things (such as how we format tables), if we typed "75%" in our proposal, that is how that text will show up in an excerpt. When we include excerpts from the grant guidelines or federal forms, we do not correct any errors that might have appeared in those excerpts in their original form.

Parting Words of Encouragement

We are confident that with this book in your hands, you can add government proposal writing to your fundraising toolbox. If you've written foundation or corporate grant proposals, you already have many of the skills you need. But even if you haven't, you can develop the skills you need to submit competitive federal applications. When you become proficient at the task, your skills will be in strong demand in an amazing variety of fields.

During lean years when fewer grant programs are offered and fewer dollars are being awarded at the federal and state levels, the competition for remaining funds will be even stiffer. You can develop the skills you need to rise to the top of this competitive swirl. We show you how.

Chapter One

How Federal Grants Work

IN THIS CHAPTER

···→ Guidelines, RFAs, and alphabet soup

···→ The federal grant life cycle

···→ How you get the good news

Before we delve into the details of how to find the right grant opportunities and how to write an excellent proposal, this chapter provides an overview of the federal grants process. You will need to understand this process to follow along with the rest of this book. We promise, no quiz at the end.

First, let's take our first foray into the world of federal alphabet soup. What grant professionals are used to calling "the guidelines" go by many names and acronyms in the government grants world. Here are some:

◆ Request for Applications (RFA)

◆ Request for Proposals (RFP)

◆ Program solicitation

◆ Notice of Funding Availability (NOFA) or Funding Opportunity (NOFO)

◆ Solicitation for Grant Applications (SGA)

◆ Broad Agency Announcement (BAA)

- ◆ Annual Program Statement (APS)

- ◆ Federal funding announcement

- ◆ Program guidance or the guidance

All of these refer to the same thing: the instructions that tell you that there is funding available and how you can win it.

In this book, we will most often refer to the guidelines or the RFA. But get to know this list and creative variations on it so you don't miss the opportunity to apply for a grant because someone called it a Funding Opportunity Announcement instead of an RFA.

The Life of a Typical Funding Opportunity

With the caveat that there can always be exceptions and that any funding agency can take its own approach, here's an overview of how federal grants usually work. Yes, we know that a lot

---

When a Grant Is Not a Grant

We oversimplify the funding landscape by calling the funding opportunities to which you respond "grants." Although you oftentimes won't notice a real difference, here's a quick overview of the differences among the most common funding vehicles you will encounter:

- ◆ *Competitive grants.* An award is considered a "grant" when the funding agency does not expect a product in return (other than the report) or does not expect to be a partner with you in delivering activities or conducting evaluation. When grants are competitive, the funding agency must announce the availability of funds and let organizations apply.

- ◆ *Cooperative agreements.* Cooperative agreements are a lot like competitive grants, but they require more interaction between the funding agency and the recipient. Sometimes this means only that the grant recipient agrees to participate in the funding agency's evaluation processes. Other times, the expectations are higher. Pay attention to the RFA's "fine print."

- ◆ *Loans and combination grants/loans.* These are just what they sound like. Some agencies loan money to recipients, usually at very favorable terms. Or the funds may come to the recipient as part grant (does not have to be paid back) and part loan (does have to be paid back and may or may not incur interest).

- ◆ *Contracts.* A federal contract is an agreement for the contractor to provide certain goods and services. It is not a grant and operates under different guidelines and regulations.

In addition, there are noncompetitive/formula grants, which are allocated by other methods and do not allow you to apply for them.

happens behind the scenes before a funding opportunity is announced, but we begin at the point at which most applicants get involved.

◆ Funding agency may announce funding opportunities that will be available later in the year. Some do this, but many do not. Agencies do their best to predict upcoming deadlines and the release of RFAs. But much can happen to affect when a grant opportunity is finally announced and a deadline set. Just do your best to keep track of when agencies anticipate releasing program guidelines by watching the agency website or subscribing to commercial services that track funding programs. If you know about an upcoming grant opportunity, you can begin planning your program and drafting your proposal based on last year's guidelines.

◆ Notice of funding opportunity and the application deadline are published in the *Federal Register* with information about how to get the complete guidelines. You may have only thirty days between the notice that an RFA is available and the submission deadline. Some grant competitions are one-time-only events. The RFA will usually make this clear. Some come out every year, while others are released in alternate years or every three or four years. It's important to know this when weighing the pros and cons of responding to a particular RFA.

> *Federal Register:* A daily publication that lists rules, public notices, and requests for proposals from all federal agencies. Available by email subscription and searchable online at federalregister.gov.
>
> *Grants.gov:* An online system for searching for grant opportunities, obtaining grant guidelines and application packages, and submitting grants. It is used by most federal agencies.

◆ Applicants download the complete RFA and application package from Grants.gov or the funder's website. In fact, we recommend scouring every resource you can find for FAQ, times of possible conference calls or webinars that may be held to give advice to applicants (usually called technical assistance), and lists of previous grantees. Don't just download the RFA and assume that you have all of the important information.

◆ Some funding agencies ask for a letter of intent (LOI) prior to the application deadline so that they have an idea of how many proposals to expect. Sometimes this is required—and you cannot submit a full proposal if you do not submit an LOI first. Other times, an LOI is optional. The RFA will tell you.

◆ Applicants submit grant applications by the deadline. We will be dissecting the grant application piece by piece in the upcoming chapters.

One of the best ways to learn about federal grants and understand how reviewers read and score your proposals is to serve as a reviewer yourself. Once you've worked a few times with a program officer who has awarded your organization a grant, you may receive an invitation to serve as a reviewer. But you don't have to wait for the pretty embossed paper. Many agencies request potential reviewers to contact them and submit their credentials. A list of these agencies is provided in **Appendix D**.

◆ The funding agency assigns grant reviewers to panels and divides grant applications among the panels. Sometimes reviewers are agency staff members. Sometimes they are recruited from previous grant recipients and other qualified people. Regardless of who is reading your proposal, your number-one job is to make each reviewer's job easy!

◆ Reviewers read and score applications. They usually have only a small window of time to read a large stack of proposals and enter scores into an online system. If they are volunteers instead of agency staff, reviewers are usually squeezing reading applications in among their own jobs, taking their kids to doctor appointments, cleaning up dog messes, and casting their votes for *Dancing with the Stars*. It's your job to make important points of your proposal stand out like flashing red lights. Otherwise, tired, overworked, but well-meaning reviewers may miss them entirely.

How Your Application Gets Scored

Officially, the decisions regarding which applications get funded are made as objectively as possible. Once reviewers are selected, they usually score proposals in groups called "panels." Their job is to grade the applications assigned to their panel and award a score to each one. This score is based on the evaluation criteria provided in the RFA.

Reviewers usually receive a scoring matrix drawn directly from the RFA's evaluation criteria. The reviewers read your proposal to ensure that you earn all of your points. They often write comments explaining why they gave you an excellent score or why they did not award you the full points for that section. Other times, you will receive no reviewer comments.

The review panels then pass their scored proposals up to the agency staff. In some situations, agency staff then have the leeway to bump applications up or down on the list according to other award criteria. Agency staff also often have the authority to reduce the final award amount of some or all grantees, and this is a common strategy to enable them to make more awards. Regardless of how the final funding list is comprised, the agency then awards grants down the list until it runs out of money.

There Is No Money Tree

We get calls, probably every week, from people who have been told that federal grants are free money, just dripping off the trees. That for-profit companies (especially if they are woman- or minority-owned) can get lots of money this way.

Oh dear. We need to debunk that "free money" concept.

◆ *Important grant truth one:* It is possible that a grant will cost your organization money. Yes, it may cost you more to implement the grant than the revenue you receive from the grant.

  Your bookkeeper will have more work tracking and reporting on the grant money. Your custodial or utilities bills may go up because of increased use of your facility. Adding staff means someone has to supervise them and increases the load on the payroll department. The executive director will spend more time than you imagined dealing with the funding agency. Sometimes your attorney or CPA needs to get involved. These costs can be heavy, especially if your organization cannot recover them in the grant as direct or indirect costs (which we will explain later).

◆ *Important grant truth two:* Federal grant money cannot replace your existing operating budget. You must do something new or expanded with your grant. Learn the mantra "supplement, not supplant." Federal grant funds may only supplement what you are doing, not take the place of your existing funds. (Yes, some ongoing programs that may be completely grant funded, like Head Start or Upward Bound, award funds to enable you to continue delivering the same services. But when the program first began, it was something new. So the federal funds did not replace your funds, at least not to deliver the same services to the same number of people.)

◆ *Important grant truth three:* More and more applicants are competing for fewer and fewer dollars. You can't just call your senator and get a check in the mail. Grants are won through a competitive, time-consuming process. You will probably pay a staff member or consultant to spend dozens and even hundreds of hours on a proposal that is a gamble. Choose carefully when deciding to submit an application, and use your resources wisely.

important

Let's say that the Big Government Agency has $1 million to award to applicants during this competition. They received 450 applications requesting a total of $5 million in funding. Clearly, only 20 percent of applications will get funded. Here's an example of how the agency decides:

Application 1: Score 100—grant request $250,000

Application 2: Score 100—grant request $200,000

Application 3: Score 99—grant request $225,000

Application 4: Score 98.8—grant request $250,000   At this point, only $75,000 left to award

Application 5: Score 98.5—grant request $200,000

Application 6: Score 98—grant request $225,000

Applicant 5 may get no award. Or the funding agency may give grants to the top five applications but require all applicants to reduce their grant budgets. Applicant 6 and all other applicants are out of luck.

While the above example is fictional, the point at which applications are cut off is right from real life. It is not unusual for highly competitive programs to have cutoff scores of 98.6 or higher.

> Most federal grant competitions are so competitive that you must earn every possible point to have a chance of winning a grant. If you realize that you are not able to earn some points—maybe because you cannot answer a certain question or perhaps because you do not meet some criterion—think again. Try to find a creative way to earn that point, or you may need to wait for another opportunity that is a better fit.

That means, in the example provided above, that any application that scores less than 98.6 will not receive funds. You can never afford to lose a single point. Be sure to take advantage of any opportunity to earn "extra credit" through competitive preferences or bonus points.

Whether you win the grant or are declined, most funding agencies have a process by which you can request a copy of your scores and the reviewers' comments. Do this whenever possible, because reading reviewers' comments can help you understand your proposal's strengths and weaknesses. If you were not funded, the reviewers' comments and your scores can help you improve your application for next time. Some program officers will even review your score sheets with you and can provide additional insight. You won't know unless you ask.

Awarding Grants

The funding agency decides which applications will receive grants. Usually this is based on the order of the points awarded by reviewers. However, agencies do have flexibility to apply other criteria to their rankings, such as geographic diversity (meaning grant dollars are spread around the country rather than being used to benefit only a few states), points awarded for previous performance, bonus points, or priorities (such as whether the applicant is in a rural location or an enterprise redevelopment zone).

The funder may notify congressional delegations of awards that will be made in their districts. If this happens, your first indication that you have won the grant may be a congratulatory call or email from your representative or senator's office. Don't worry if you don't hear from your delegation. Not every agency notifies them.

If your organization is selected to receive a grant, the funding agency sends a letter or email. This is usually called a Notice of Grant Award (NGA) or something similar. This notification confirms that you were selected to receive an award, assigns an award number, and includes other such details as the starting and ending dates of the grant period and the amount awarded. It may also explain reporting requirements, but if it does not, we tell you later how these requirements might be specified by the agency.

Your organization may have to sign an agreement and return it or other documents to the funding agency before the grant becomes official. Sometimes the program officer (an agency staff member assigned to this funding program) contacts you to renegotiate parts of your budget, especially if you were awarded less than you requested. The agency sometimes even wants you to change your project activities or objectives. Usually this is fine. However, consider

---

When Do You Get the Money?

You know how when you get a foundation grant, you usually get a check for the entire grant right up front? Well, federal grants are not like that, as one organization we know learned the hard way.

The organization was still pretty new to federal grants. It was definitely used to the "you got the grant; here's your money" model. After receiving its federal Notice of Grant Award, the organization got all set up on the electronic system through which it was to request the grant funds be deposited into its bank account.

Then the organization downloaded its money for the year. All of it.

No one realized (yes, we're sure it was in the fine print somewhere) that you're supposed to spread out your requests during the year—say quarterly. And it's really hard to put the money back once you've taken it out.

There were some annoyed calls from the funding agency to the grantee, lots of groveling, and promises all the way up to the organization's president that the grantee would spend every penny appropriately and have the world's best documentation behind every expenditure.

That was a lesson that stuck! Everyone dealing with money at that organization knew, in the future, to request partial payments at intervals throughout the year—after the funds had been spent. After a year or two of good behavior, the red flag was removed from the organization's account with the funding agency, but it was certainly stressful when it happened.

stories from the real world

all such requests carefully and make sure you can meet them. If not, it is better to reject the grant at this stage than to take on something that you can't achieve or that jeopardizes the organization's finances.

Once your organization is selected to receive a federal grant, you will be assigned to a program officer at the funding agency. This is a very important person to get to know. Contact the program officer as soon as possible to begin building that relationship. Ask about communication preferences. Are emails or phone calls preferred? Some program officers appreciate periodic anecdotal information about your project. Some only want the reports to be filed on time. And filing reports on time is critical.

We know this life cycle is oversimplified, but it hits the highlights most relevant to those responsible for preparing proposals. Focus on what is within your control—designing an excellent program and producing a top-notch proposal. While there will always be some factors beyond your control (such as how an agency decides to distribute funds around the country or whether a reviewer on your panel did not read your proposal carefully), an excellent proposal gives you the best chance of success.

To Recap

◆ RFAs go by many different names. Getting to know those terms can help you avoid missing an opportunity to apply for funding.

◆ Focus your energy on submitting the best proposals possible.

◆ Receiving the word that you won the grant is only the beginning. It's not unusual to be required to adjust project activities, your planned outcomes, or the budget as a condition of the award.

Chapter Two

Are We Ready for Federal Grants?

IN THIS CHAPTER

···→ Assessing your capacity to implement and manage a grant

···→ Assessing your capacity to prepare proposals

···→ Working ahead so that you are ready to apply

It is a truth universally acknowledged that executive directors or board members in search of new revenue are in want of federal grants. Or so we think Jane Austen might have said if she had made her living as a grant writer rather than a novelist. However, it is also true that board members or bosses sometimes may have less insight into the qualities that will guarantee a good match between your organization and the right funding sources, just like parents may not always recognize the mate who will be best for you.

Federal grants can bring your organization many benefits. They can help you start or continue important programs, sometimes for years at a time. They can give you credibility with other funders. Federal grants can increase access to education or health care or the arts for underserved populations. One federal grant may far outstrip the amount you have raised from all other funders for years. In short, they can be a vital force for addressing the social problems you get out of bed every morning to solve.

With that in mind, we are still firm believers in looking before leaping. Yes, federal grants can bring in lots of money. But they are also complicated and cumbersome—at the application stage, but even more importantly, during the implementation and reporting stages.

Before you dive into writing a time-consuming proposal, take an honest and comprehensive look at your organization's readiness and capacity to both win and manage federal grants.

Federal Grants and Faith-Based Organizations

Faith-based organizations provide many essential services in our communities, such as food pantries, disaster relief, after-school programs, and assistance to veterans and the homeless. These organizations are part of the fabric of our communities.

And they are fully eligible for federal grants. We have successfully won federal grants for a range of faith-based organizations. Just remember, you can spend federal funds only on services to the community, not on religious activities.

Sometimes faith-based organizations fear that accepting federal funds will require them to change their hiring practices, remove religious symbols or artwork, or change their names. These fears are unfounded. It is true that you must be cautious when making announcements about worship services or religious study. You can let program participants know such activities are available, but be careful not to create a situation in which you imply they are required.

Of course, there are some reasonable restrictions. You may not use federal grant funds for actual religious activities such as worship, prayer, proselytizing, or study of religious texts for religious purposes. Nor can you require recipients of services funded by federal dollars to participate in religious activities or refuse to serve clients on the basis of their religion or their participation in religious activities outside the grant-funded program. But that's it. Those are really the only limitations.

Let us tell you the story of one church that receives federal funds to supplement its community meals program. The church is not required to cover or remove its crosses, stained glass windows, or pictures in the Sunday school rooms. Bibles do not have to be hidden away. The church doesn't need to do anything to hide the fact that it is a church.

Program staff and volunteers start their day before participants arrive with prayer. When people arrive at the church for their meal, they are warmly greeted by a pastor, who is dressed in his usual clerical attire. Participants hear announcements about other services such as visiting nurses, representatives from Veterans Affairs who are coming next week, Bible study on Wednesday evening, and a blanket distribution led by the women's guild.

When the meal is served, the pastor or a volunteer offers a moment of silence. After their meal, participants select from donated clothing and personal hygiene items while a member of the clergy visits informally with them.

This example is a picture-perfect execution of what faith-based organizations do and do so well—and all of it is fully consistent with federal requirements.

We hear many concerns that "federal funds will change the way we do business." While receiving a federal grant may significantly impact your accounting practices or purchasing policies, and you cannot discriminate among those who receive your services, little else should be affected.

If you have concerns about your rights and obligations under a particular funding opportunity, talk with an attorney familiar with federal law, such as the First Amendment and other relevant civil rights legislation. Many federal funding agencies and the White House Office of Faith-based and Neighborhood Partnerships also provide guidance to faith-based organizations seeking funding (whitehouse.gov/administration/eop/ofbnp).

Don't let the fact that you are a faith-based organization scare you away from seeking federal grants. Sometimes there is no one better equipped in your community to provide food, shelter, day care, counseling, education, or substance-abuse services than your organization. If federal funds will help you expand your services to more people in need, go for it.

important

In fact, examine your organization's ability to properly implement a federal grant-funded program before considering if you can write the proposal. You may have the capacity to write a stunning grant proposal, but if you lack the ability to deliver the promised activities, there is no reason to bother.

Capacity to Implement, Manage, and Report on a Federal Grant

You may be thinking, "If we are getting a grant to implement this project, don't the grant funds give us enough capacity to do it?" Not exactly. Evaluate anything that can positively (or negatively) affect your organization's ability to manage a government grant.

Here are some key questions to ask yourself to help determine your organization's capacity for implementing, managing, and reporting on a federal grant:

- *Cash flow.* Do you have enough cash on hand to wait to be reimbursed for grant expenses? Many federal grants require recipients to spend their own funds on the grant expenses and then wait for reimbursement. Can you pay personnel and meet other project expenses while waiting, perhaps months, to be reimbursed by the funding agency? If your budget is tight, it's a good idea to find out how and when you will receive the funds from the agency to which you wish to apply.

- *Accounting practices.* Can you track grant funds separately from the organization's general budget? Using the features of accounting software, such as account numbers, classes, or departments, is an effective way to do this.

- *Track record.* How long have you been in existence and serving the community? It's pretty rare for a brand-new organization to win a federal grant if it has no track record of serving its target population. Some agencies require that you have two or three years of audited financials

A social service organization that we know of was considering applying for a grant that would require extensive reporting on demographic data. With a small administrative staff, this organization did not have the capacity to track and analyze the required data. In fact, compiling the statistics would have required the organization to purchase software and invest staff time—expenses that could not be covered by the grant.

In addition, the grant would have required more hours from the organization's part-time bookkeeper to compile grant reports. This expense was also not allowed to be included in the grant budget.

You won't be surprised, then, when we tell you that this organization did the math and realized it would cost more to operate the grant than the grant would bring in. Making the decision not to apply was the logical choice and saved that organization from making a decision that could have threatened its finances instead of strengthened them.

stories from the real world

on hand before you can apply. What data or other information can you provide that demonstrates that you know what you're doing and are making a difference in the community?

◆ *Personnel.* If you plan to reassign existing personnel to grant activities, how will you cover their former duties? If you will hire staff for the grant's project, ensure that you can attract qualified personnel with competitive pay and benefits and that you have an effective recruitment plan. Sometimes smaller nonprofits and those located in rural areas have challenges attracting staff, so be honest about your true capacity in this area.

◆ *Clear goals.* Do you have a strategic plan or clear goals that your board has adopted? Are these goals guiding your decisions about programs and which federal grants to pursue? Do not let the dazzle of big money lure you into mission creep. Remember, grants should serve the needs of your programs, not the other way around.

Mission creep: The tendency to pursue funding or begin projects that go beyond the organization's mission.

(d)(e)finition

◆ *Space.* If you are going to hire people to deliver grant activities, do you have offices for them? If you are not allowed to pay for furniture from the grant, do you have desks and chairs for the new personnel? If you ramp up the number people to be served, are your facilities adequate to handle them?

◆ *Data tracking.* What capacity do you have to count the people who receive grant-funded services and record all manner of information about those people? You don't have to have an expensive database. But you need some way of collecting and recording the data that will be needed for evaluation and reporting purposes. Who will be responsible for collecting and tracking participant data, and how will you manage the data?

These are the basics, the foundational elements all applicants should have in place. We're sure you can think of others that may be unique to your situation or your type of organization. The point is to go into a potential application with eyes wide open. We don't want you to fall victim to an unfortunate surprise.

Capacity to Prepare an Application

Okay. You're feeling ready. You've assessed your organization and determined you can accept the challenge of managing a federal grant. Now consider what resources you can devote to preparing an application.

Time

Most federal proposals take hundreds of hours to develop—once you consider the time of everyone involved. If you are new to federal grants, we recommend following that old strategy taught to beginning consultants and lawyers: "Calculate how much time this case (or project) will take. Got it? Now double that estimate, and you might be close."

One of the first questions for yourself when assessing your capacity to apply for federal grants should be, "Can our staff devote that much time between now and the grant deadline to preparing the proposal?" If you've stumbled upon a grant opportunity that is due in two weeks, the answer is probably no. Even if there are thirty days to write the proposal, the answer may still be no.

Project Planning

Writing is the easy part. A writer has to have something to write about. Even the most experienced grant professional will require hours and hours for planning, gathering data, attending meetings, researching statistics, exploring partnerships, confirming information, and developing a strong budget before a single word can be written.

Pulling the Plug

We use that visual image whenever we talk about starting a grant application only to decide we can't pursue it after all.

Cheryl once worked with an organization that was a perfect fit for an upcoming grant to provide capacity building to other nonprofits. Planning meetings began in earnest, mapping out the activities and deciding how to staff the project.

But when it came time to get the details behind the budget figures, the whole thing fell apart. The applicant realized it would not be allowed to "make a profit." From the organization's perspective, there was no benefit to expanding its outreach and staff for a temporary period of time if the grant funds had no impact on the financial bottom line.

It's better to pull the plug, even if you have already started an application, than to keep moving forward with a grant that may stress your organization if you actually win it.

stories from the real world

Who is the best person at your organization to plan all of the details of (usually) a multiyear project? The project may affect more than one department or area of your organization. It will likely have long-term impacts on the people you serve or how or where you serve them. Big decisions will have to be made.

The skills required to prepare a successful federal proposal far exceed writing ability alone. A tremendous amount of thinking and strategy informs your writing, and you need time to design a strong project.

food for thought

Senior Leadership

Because of all the possible impacts on personnel, the organization's future direction, finances, and collaborative relationships within the community, smaller organizations especially need their top leaders at the table.

Organizations of all sizes need to keep senior leadership informed and will need their full support of the project.

In smaller organizations, "senior leadership" may be only one person, such as the executive director. At other organizations, the board may need to pass a resolution approving applying for a grant, especially if it requires matching funds or other promises from the applicant. Sometimes the RFA requires evidence of board approval.

In larger organizations, the senior leadership role may be filled by a dean or vice president. It's not the title that matters. What matters is that you have the support of someone with authority to make decisions that may change the organization for years to come. Usually that's not the grant professional, development director, or program staff.

Can You Be Too Small for a Federal Grant?

"Are we too small to compete for a federal grant?" That question comes up now and then. The answer is no. We know of organizations that had no staff—only board members—that have successfully won planning grants from federal agencies.

The executive director of a nonprofit in suburban Maryland shared with us his story of how his organization won its first federal grant. The organization was young, only about three years old. It did have five people on staff, but with so much work to do, only two could be freed up to work on the grant proposal.

An opportunity arose to reply to an RFP from the Substance Abuse and Mental Health Services Administration (SAMHSA) for a planning grant. It was perfect. The funds would pay for something that was a priority for the organization. The staff knew their chances of winning were small. There were going to be only forty-two grants awarded, not even one per state. At this time, the organization was located in Washington, DC. You may be surprised to hear this can actually work against applicants, because Congress wants to see funds spread out throughout the country.

They knew they would be competing with larger organizations with bigger budgets. But the staff, who had never written a federal proposal, put their "heart and soul" into the application, the executive director told us. One of the founders helped by scanning the entire proposal to ensure that every single detail was correct.

Their proposal earned one of the highest scores, and the organization had its first federal grant under its belt. This organization has since gone on to win multiple grants from local, state, and federal sources, as well as from foundations. The executive director tells us federal grants feel "less political" than local grants, but we are convinced one reason this organization is so successful in its grant seeking is because the executive director remains closely involved in all federal applications.

stories from the real world

Project Management

We recommend treating the application itself as a project to be managed. It has timelines. It has dependencies. For example, you can't write about the project until the program people tell you what services they are planning to deliver.

One of our grants colleagues who has an engineering background creates a Gantt chart of all tasks and milestones related to finishing the application and getting it submitted on time. While the English major among your two authors breaks out in hives at the very thought, we both agree that you need some system of shepherding proposals to completion.

Find the person in your organization who is absolutely compulsive about details. You know those people who annoy you when you all go out to lunch because they can't help but correct typographical errors on the menu? Or are frustrated every time they see a sign advertising "CD's?" You want that person on your team double- and triple-checking that you have pulled together all of the forms, that they're signed by the right person, and that the proposal's formatting follows the rules in the guidelines.

> Our best advice about getting information you need from your colleagues? Tell them you need the content or documents well before the application deadline. You will spend a lot of time waiting on others. Waiting for them to sign forms, or tell you how many people the project will serve, or confirm what their supplies will cost. Most people will be late. They will forget. Something will get lost in someone's inbox. Give people your request, be specific about when you need it done, but ask for it well before your true drop-dead time. Believe us, you will need every bit of that "padding."

 practical tip

Writing

We purposefully left writing for last. Writing is important. Think of the word "proposal." It conjures up a scary conversation, one that is rife with the possibility of rejection. If the right message is not communicated correctly, an otherwise excellent relationship may never move forward. How stressful.

If you don't have a grant professional on staff, then deputize someone who is (1) a good writer, (2) detail oriented, (3) patient, (4) a good team player, (5) persistent, and (6) thick skinned. Then complement that person with a project leader or program design lead who has (1) excellent facilitation skills, (2) the ability to think strategically and long term, and (3) the authority to obtain the necessary information or organization-wide decisions for the proposal content.

In some organizations, these roles can be capably filled by the same person. Sometimes it makes sense to divide these responsibilities among different people. There is no "right" way to organize the proposal preparation team—other than to assign the best people you can who can work together effectively to get the job done.

Pre-Positioning Yourself to Compete

If you're like us, you are always running from one deadline to the next. Things don't get done until they're urgent because something else has to get done first.

However, set aside a little time to complete some tasks that will have you ready ahead of time to apply. Then you can focus your energies and brainpower on the application itself when it's time to work on the proposal. If you can tackle just one of the items below each week, you'll chip away at this to-do list and be prepared to respond quickly to funding opportunities when they come open.

"Why haven't you talked about our 501(c)(3) status? Shouldn't that be top of our list for capacity?"

Actually, not necessarily. Some grants are awarded to organizations that are registered as nonprofits in their states but do not hold 501(c)(3) status. In some rare cases, even for-profit companies are eligible. Take a look at the "eligibility" section of previous grant guidelines for the programs of most interest to your organization. The RFA will state quite clearly whether for-profits or nonprofits without 501(c)(3) status are eligible.

Registrations and Accounts

While there are a few exceptions, most federal agencies require all applicants to be registered in the online systems called Grants.gov and the System for Award Management (SAM). Actually, there are at least three separate registrations to complete before you are ready to submit a grant application. It can take a while between registration steps for the next step to be activated. If you know you are going to apply for a federal grant sometime in the next year, get registered on Grants.gov now. **Appendix C** has easy-to-follow instructions for this so you can cross it off your list. Of course, websites change frequently. Be sure to check the Grants.gov website for the most current instructions when you start your registration.

If you are not comfortable completing semicomplex tasks online, filling in form fields, and uploading attachments, find yourself a techie friend. Gone are the days of staying up until three in the morning, standing at Kinko's making and binding ten hard copies of your grant application, and driving all night to deliver them to Washington, DC, before the deadline (or spending a fortune on FedEx). And, boy, are we glad those days are gone.

Of course, you may still be up until three in the morning. But you might be spending that time converting documents to PDF, trying to upload your attachments, and watching the Grants. gov servers spin while they try to process your application. Sometimes those late nights are unavoidable.

Technology

You don't have to be a techie whiz kid to prepare federal applications, but some basic technology resources and knowledge will smooth the process considerably.

Make sure you have the resources or can access a partner, volunteer, or consultant who can help you with the following:

◆ A high-speed Internet connection for uploading your application to the funder

◆ An email address to provide for the required point of contact at your organization

◆ Software that lets you convert documents into PDF format, required by some applications and recommended for most others

◆ A scanner for getting older documents, such as your 501(c)(3) letter or your Articles of Incorporation, into electronic format for submission with your application, and software that allows you to edit PDF files

◆ The ability to create basic charts (can be as basic as simple boxes with text in them, connected by lines), needed for making organizational charts and logic models

◆ The ability to manipulate numbers in a spreadsheet, using formulas to calculate totals and percentages, needed for creating and frequently editing your budget so that any changes automatically update all totals and subtotals

Partnerships

Some grant programs require applicants to apply as partners or as a consortium of several partners. Take some time now to consider who your natural partners are, and reach out to ask them to consider joining you on a future application. Calling up another organization when the application is due in two weeks and asking them to commit resources to your project is usually not a positive start to a good relationship.

Register Early to Avoid Heartache

Karen once worked with a small organization (only two people on staff). The organization thought it had completed all of the steps to register through Grants.gov—only to find out it had never been assigned a CAGE (Commercial and Government Entity) code. Yes, it was literally stuck in a CAGE process.

Now, as funny as being stuck in a CAGE might sound, the grant was due in less than a week. So while Karen was working to complete a complex grant proposal, the organization was unsure it would even be able to submit the proposal. Talk about stressful!

In the end, everything worked out, but not until the day before the deadline. We recommend getting the Grants.gov and SAM registration processes out of the way before you have a deadline. But if you can't, have someone stay on top of the process so that you can submit that proposal you worked so hard on.

 stories from the real world

Written Expectations—A Road Map for Successful Partnerships

A colleague of ours is the executive director of an organization that has been asked to partner on two federal grants. One partnership experience was a nightmare, while the other is going smoothly.

Both partnerships originated with grant applicants who were required to have domestic violence organizations as partners to be eligible for funding. The partnership that did not survive resulted from a grant applicant calling two local domestic violence organizations and asking them to be a partner on a Department of Justice Safe Havens grant. The organizations had no previous relationship. While there was a written Memorandum of Understanding (MOU), it was vague and did not clearly spell out each partner's roles and responsibilities in the grant project. By the time the grant was awarded, the personnel at all three agencies had changed. Our colleague described it as "mass confusion," as no one knew who was supposed to contribute what services or expertise. Ultimately, the applicant had to return the grant to the Department of Justice and lost a real opportunity to make a difference in the lives of its clients.

Just down the road, another applicant for an Administration for Children and Families Healthy Marriages grant also needed a domestic violence organization as a partner. That applicant also called our colleague's organization. Even though no MOU was executed, expectations regarding scope of work were communicated in writing between the organizations. Once the grant was awarded, the domestic violence organization requested written confirmation of the services it was expected to provide under the grant. Expectations were clear and limited and communicated clearly. That partnership continues to function as planned.

Organizational Information and Documents

Start with the information you need to apply for any grant, and make yourself a profile sheet of your organization that has all of its vital information, such as the address, fax number, web address, tax number, full legal name, and so on. Scan in your IRS letter, and request a digital copy of your audit from your auditors.

We've created a checklist for you of items like these to collect in support of future grant applications. Gather them now. You're going to need them anyway. See **Appendix E**.

There are other resources from within your organization that you will find incredibly useful because you can mine them for proposal content. It is not likely you will actually have to include any of them in their entirety in a proposal. But you will find yourself frequently drawing upon the items provided in the table on the next page to support your application. You can use information drawn from these sources in multiple proposal sections, such as organizational capacity or the need section.

Documents Used to Support Proposal Preparation

Internal Documents	Common Uses
Strategic plan (current, no more than three to five years old, with evidence it is updated regularly)	◆ To develop the program goals and objectives ◆ To demonstrate that proposed project is an organizational priority
Annual report	◆ May contain data to support case for need ◆ Evidence of previous successes can be used to support program plans or evaluation design ◆ Can also demonstrate capacity of the organization to design and deliver projects similar in scope or complexity to the proposed project
Evaluation reports	◆ Can demonstrate capacity to measure outcomes and achieve results ◆ May contain data that supports the case for need ◆ Also demonstrates organization is successful at delivering projects similar in scope or complexity to the proposed project
Newsletters, program brochures, and other informational publications	◆ Good sources of content to describe the organization, its mission, and the people it serves ◆ Typically include good summaries of major programs ◆ May have some history of the organization, such as when and why it was founded
Previous grant proposals	◆ Useful for describing the population served by the organization ◆ Often can inform the content of any section of the federal proposal

Such documents, along with established partnerships and active registrations on federal submission websites, will position the grant professional on your team to jump right in to preparing a competitive proposal.

As we have discussed, the person primarily responsible for the grant application may be a staff member, volunteer, or consultant. Regardless, this person cannot be successful working alone or in a silo. The grant professional needs the support of several other people to complete the process. That's why the next chapter tells you how to build your grants dream team.

To Recap

◆ Federal grants are great and can make your organization stronger. But don't chase the money. Stick with your mission and what you do well. Avoid mission creep.

◆ Assess your capacity to implement and manage a grant-funded project before trying to decide if you can write a proposal.

◆ Complete your Grants.gov and SAM registrations as early as possible so that you are able to submit your proposal on time.

◆ Be realistic about the time required to develop a strong grant proposal and about the number of people who will need to be involved.

Chapter Three

Building Your Grants Dream Team

IN THIS CHAPTER

···→ The benefits of a team-based approach

···→ Who should be on your grants team

···→ Adding a consultant to your team

We know that those reading this book work in an array of environments. Some of you are at large organizations, such as major hospital systems or universities that have multiple administrative offices that can support your grant-seeking work. Others of you are at small organizations. Maybe you feel as if there is no grants "team." Maybe you are the executive director, development director, grant professional, and janitor all in one.

We are aware of this, and this chapter addresses issues unique to both ends of the size spectrum. Large organizations often have grants committees that meet regularly to recommend which grants to apply for and may even collaborate on preparing the applications. In higher education, government grants may be sought by one office (sponsored programs), with grant seeking from foundations and corporations handled by the development office.

For smaller organizations, the "team" may be your entire staff. We've seen teams that were no larger than an executive director and a part-time administrative assistant who comprised the entire staff. Don't forget that you can tap board members or other volunteers. For example, the board treasurer may be your equivalent of "the finance office." In some ways, being small allows you to be more nimble. Fewer people have to weigh in on each decision, meaning you often have more flexibility to be creative or innovative. So don't get discouraged if you are at a smaller organization. Small organizations regularly win government grants.

Regardless of your organization's size or complexity, developing a "dream team" of committed members helps lighten the load at every stage of acquiring and managing federal grants.

The Deciding to Apply Stage

Even large organizations often do not have the personnel or the time to apply for every grant they might be interested in. Especially if multiple grants require the organization to raise or otherwise contribute additional funds to the project (called "matching funds"), it may not be financially feasible to operate several grants at a time. In that case, grant opportunities have to be prioritized.

Develop a simple one-page form that summarizes the key information about each grant opportunity for decision makers. That way, grants are being evaluated on the same criteria—apples to apples—whenever possible. After a few years, you will have a valuable collection of grants information that can help inform future decisions. See *Writing to Win Federal Grants–The Workbook* for a few samples of such forms.

 practical tip

The decision whether to apply might be made by the executive director, a small leadership team, or a large cross-departmental grants committee. Regardless, a team-based approach helps overcome internal politics and helps ensure that decisions regarding which grants to pursue are made on the basis of what is best for the entire organization.

Whoever decides whether or not you will apply should use a set of objective criteria to decide which grant opportunities to pursue. This makes the decision-making process more effective, justifies decisions to stakeholders, and educates your team members as they learn to apply the criteria to grant decisions. The more people at every level of your organization who understand government grants, the easier your job will be.

The Application Stage

Once you make a yes decision on a particular grant opportunity, you often have to move very quickly to meet the deadline. While the grant professional is usually the best person to do most of the work on the grant proposal, no one can do it alone. Whoever is writing the grant will need information, approvals, and data from multiple offices, departments, or people. If you are the grant professional, develop good relationships with these people. You will depend on them.

The typical participants on a grants dream team include the grant professional (and perhaps others in the development department), program staff, finance staff, and human resources staff. Other contributors may join the team or be invited at relevant times (such as the facilities director if you are pursuing a capital grant). At small organizations, the same person may fill multiple roles. The number of people present is not as important as having access to the information you need.

While organizations are different and may use different titles for certain positions or departments, the chart below summarizes the most common contributors to a winning proposal.

Department or Person	Responsibilities and Contributions to Federal Proposals
Development office	Identifies funding prospects, coordinates proposal development, writes content, seeks data, manages the submission process, commits to raising any required matching funds, ensures adherence to guidelines
Program staff or principal investigator	Identifies need in community for program (data and anecdotes), provides subject-matter expertise, designs program activities, provides budget costs, develops program logic model, determines desired outcomes, sets performance objectives
Finance office	Helps with and confirms budget numbers, provides copies of audits and financial statements, helps articulate "other costs" of delivering the program, may identify resources to leverage, may provide salary and fringe benefits data in absence of an HR office
Human resources office or outsourced HR/payroll	Reviews project staff plan, identifies any staffing issues (such as staff-to-participant ratios, percentage of effort, etc.), provides salary data, calculates the fringe benefits rate, provides description of how personnel are recruited and hired
Executive director or board chair	Signs federal certifications and assurances, may seek board approval, may confer with legal counsel regarding regulations
Executive director or other senior leader, such as a vice president or director	Approves proposal and proposal budget, approves plan to staff program, approves plans to use facilities for the program, approves plans to raise matching funds or leverage organizational resources

Certain types of organizations will have additional contributors that are more specialized. For example, in higher education, an institutional research office provides large amounts of essential data about students required for educational grant proposals. Other applicants bring in an external evaluator or researcher to help design a strong evaluation plan.

Build the people on whom you will need to depend into a team that supports grant seeking as a major organizational priority. Even if most work is conducted via email and conference calls, just having group accountability can sometimes help move slower individuals along.

When you need information or content from your team members, we recommend providing them samples they can follow. Give them a model of the information you will need to include in your text. Share a sample budget that fits into federal budget categories. Most people find it less intimidating to modify an existing table or chart than to come up with one on their own.

In organizations less experienced with federal grants, sometimes the grant professional is the person who best understands logic models, allowable costs, or measurable outcomes. It can seem risky to ask others to produce these, especially since you so often have to redo them yourself. But your team members will develop their skills as you work on proposals together. With a little investment of your time and patience, they will be able to contribute more to future applications. It is also important that you cultivate their buy-in to smooth the way for even more effective program implementation after receiving the grant.

Don't expect your colleagues to create content from scratch, particularly if they have limited experience with the requirements of federal grant proposals. In fact, most people are vastly reassured if you promise they can send you bullet points or phrases instead of polished prose. Let everyone know that any text they give you will be edited so that it sounds like one person wrote the document and not twenty. This can head off resistance to your editing from those who see themselves as writers while putting at ease those who are intimidated by writing.

My Boss Expects Me to Do It All

Okay. We've convinced you that bringing other people in to the process, while sometimes messy, pays great dividends in the long run. However, maybe you have coworkers who resent that they have to help you do what they see as your work. Or maybe your boss thinks you are wasting time in meetings and should just "go write."

What? This has never happened to you? Congratulations! Never change jobs, because you are in heaven.

If you work anywhere short of heaven, sooner or later, this is going to happen to you. In the short term, we have found an incredibly effective way to drive home the point that we need important information from other people is to send our boss a draft of our proposal.

A draft with lots of holes in it. Each hole should be highlighted and accompanied by a note that says something like, "here we need the number of clients we served every year from 2009 through 2012."

This approach can help remedy either situation. It helps a boss understand why you need to involve other staff members, and it can help your boss see the need to motivate colleagues who are dragging their feet. Nothing spurs a boss into action faster than the prospect of failing to win a big grant.

Ask your colleagues to review and edit your proposal. Invite them to a meeting to go through edits. You can then steer the discussion away from typos and wordsmithing and toward the big issues. But if you take this approach to generate staff buy-in, schedule that review meeting well in advance of the submission deadline.

Once the urgency of the grant deadline is over, you can review the application process and use it to illustrate the need for everyone's contributions. Suggest that getting together at the beginning of the process is probably more efficient. Share examples of how it works elsewhere.

In the interest of building long-term productive relationships with your colleagues, try to avoid bringing in your boss or theirs until absolutely necessary. Sometimes all it takes is a "rah, rah" speech by the boss to help everyone understand what a wonderful opportunity getting this grant will be and how everyone will benefit.

Remember we said to set internal deadlines with plenty of padding? You always need time to reformat materials that you get from others or to correct errors before you incorporate the information into your final draft. Even your attachments usually have to comply with rules about font size and margins, and those you receive from others, such as resumes, often have to be reformatted to comply.

 practical tip

Being courteous also goes a long way. Don't wait until the last minute to ask for information if you don't have to. Give people reasonable deadlines, thank them sincerely, and brag about their contributions. People who feel appreciated and who feel you understand they are swamped too are more likely to help you during those times when you've got to have something from them yesterday.

Bribery works well too. It's amazing, but a nice batch of homemade chocolate chip cookies at a meeting motivates people to show up with their homework done. We know one grants officer who kept a dish of chocolate just inside her door so that program people would stop by. It was her way of making herself more approachable and developing relationships with people with whom she needed to work on grant projects.

The Management Team Saves the Day

In the table below, we have provided you with some real-life examples of potential major errors that were averted because a management team was used in the process of designing the grant project. The left-hand column tells the story of what happened when staff members went it alone when developing major proposal components. The right-hand column illustrates how having a grants team resolved the issue before it was an emergency.

Lone Ranger Danger	Dream Team Saves the Day
Program staff members try to determine costs of facilities to deliver activities. Lack of knowledge of licensing requirements led to a vast underestimate of the true facilities cost.	Facilities staff members were knowledgeable of state and local licensing requirements and also about availability of existing facilities. They were able to recommend a partnership that reduced costs.

Lone Ranger Danger	Dream Team Saves the Day
A new member of the finance staff believes a tight program budget can be stretched by not adhering strictly to required staff-to-participant ratios.	Program staff members understand regulations and how finance's proposal put the program at risk of losing its accreditation. They were able to suggest other cost-cutting measures instead.
Human resources staff members learn about new regulations that affect staff to be hired, but lack of a management team allowed this critical information to inadvertently not get communicated to grants or program staff.	Implementing a management team approach, with regular meetings and communications, ensured that all future such information would be communicated immediately to those planning grant projects.

But I Hate Group Work

If you are an overachiever or just a hard worker, you may have learned to dread processes that rely on teams to get important work done. We aren't saying that moving your organization's grant seeking culture to a management team approach is easy. We are saying that, in the long run, the approach is well worth the effort and will benefit the organization in many ways beyond its grant seeking.

We know that you regularly discover grant opportunities that appear to be a perfect fit for your organization's mission. But when you try to get the planning team on board or get buy-in from the program staff, there are other priorities or a lack of resources to commit to planning the project.

It's very tempting in these situations to jump in anyway as a Lone Ranger. You want your organization to win this grant, and you know it would help accomplish great things in your community.

We strongly recommend against taking sole responsibility for making the decision to apply or for designing the project. We have learned over the years that you can't force a grant down your colleagues' throats.

Don't get us wrong. Someone is ultimately responsible for ensuring the proposal is completed on time and accurately. But a grant professional who is supported by a talented team, with all members pulling their weight, is less likely to be stressed and exhausted at the time of submission. That can make all the difference between submitting a perfect proposal or making a fatal mistake.

Bringing a Consultant onto Your Team

Help! We get this call a lot. The grant writer is on maternity leave. We have three grants due at the same time. We've never written a federal grant. We don't know how this agency works, even though we've won lots of other grants. We have no grant writer.

Those are just some of the reasons organizations bring in consultants for their federal proposals, even when they have an experienced grants team. If you are considering consulting help for your federal grants, the Puget Sound Grantwriters Association has provided a short, helpful article on how to hire a grant consultant at grantwriters.org/how-to-hire-a-freelancer. See **Appendix F** for a list of tips on selecting the right consultant for your organization.

We will just add our own piece of advice: Contact a consultant as early as you can. Don't wait for the RFA to come out. Good consultants are often booked months in advance, and the shorter the time between your call and the application deadline, the higher the fee will likely be.

Grant consultants charge an hourly rate or a project fee that is due upon completion of the application. The fee is based on the amount of time and effort the consultant expects to spend to develop your proposal. Rates can vary significantly because they are influenced by many factors, such as whether the organization and consultant have a preexisting relationship, the consultant's location and experience, how busy the consultant may be, and how much time is left before the deadline.

Most grant consultants, particularly those who belong to professional organizations with codes of ethics, are not allowed to accept compensation for preparing your proposal out of the proceeds of the grant itself. The majority of federal agencies prohibit using grant funds to pay for any costs you incur before the grant period begins. These are known as preaward costs. In

---

Don't Go It Alone

An executive director pushed the grant writer to write a proposal for the director's pet program idea. However, other organizational staff did not see it as their job to become involved with grants. The grant writer was forced to design the project in a vacuum.

When the grant was awarded, did the organization celebrate? Did the grant writer receive a glowing performance review? No. In fact, the program staff resented that the grant required them to do "extra work." The finance director was annoyed because the grant made his job harder. Then the executive director quit. From then on, every problem with the grant was somehow the grant writer's fault. He was the only one left with any investment in the program succeeding.

As a result, the organization missed achieving several of its outcomes in the first year. Not surprisingly, the second year of funding was not authorized. A new executive director came on board who blamed the grant writer completely. The grant writer finally took a position with another organization.

So what does this example teach us? It illustrates that even though it takes work to build a management team approach, it's much riskier to try to do it all yourself. We know it will take time to help your organization come to understand that it's everyone's job to produce strong proposals.

 stories from the real world

fact, it is unethical, and possibly illegal, to divert funds out of the grant budget and spend them on something else.

We have learned over the decades that if an organization does not have the resources to pay a staff person or consultant for professional grant preparation, that organization is probably not financially stable enough to manage a federal grant anyway.

To Recap

◆ Grant professionals depend on their colleagues for important data and information. Work on building those relationships.

◆ The grants team approach can help obtain critical buy-in from those who must deliver the grant activities and avoid potentially serious problems.

◆ Communicating early and often, giving clear deadlines, and providing models can help your colleagues help you.

◆ In the end, you are responsible for the grant quality and submission, so leave yourself enough time to finish the project in time!

Chapter Four

Finding The Best Match: Prospect Research

IN THIS CHAPTER

- ···→ Start with your peers

- ···→ Mine funding agency websites

- ···→ Search free public grant lists

- ···→ Other strategies

L et's be honest. Most of us hate searching for federal grants. But with a few tips under your belt, you won't have to labor through search results of three hundred, five hundred, or even eight hundred funding opportunities just to find the one or two that might be a match.

In fact, we usually do not recommend beginning your search for federal grants with Grants.gov. Grants.gov has its strengths, but keyword searching is not one of them. You will end up there, but we begin the path elsewhere.

Steal Everyone Else's Funders

Your competitors/partners/colleagues are your best sources for funding prospects. It's not like you are luring an individual donor away from the other organization across town. But look around. If you support farmers, what federal grants have been won by other organizations like yours? Just as with foundation grants, the best indicator of which grants you are most likely to be eligible for and have a chance of winning will be the grants your colleagues at similar organizations are winning.

If there are membership organizations for people who do what you do (rural health networks, Christian colleges, children's museums), their newsletters, websites, and conferences often

If your organization is not eligible for a grant but a consortium is, sometimes your membership organization can apply for the grant on behalf of members. Be sure to find out what it takes to be invited to be part of such a grant. You will gain valuable experience with receiving and managing federal funds without having to be the applicant.

announce grant opportunities of interest to their members. Take advantage of message boards, electronic mailing lists, and conferences to ask your peers if they know of any government grants to support what you do. For example, a state health department might be eligible to receive federal funds to support tobacco-cessation programs and will need program delivery partners from inside the state to participate in the application.

Dig into the Funding Agencies

Next, think about the funding agencies most likely to fund what you do. Visit their websites. Most have sections dedicated to grants, or you can search for the word "grants" on their sites. **Appendix B** conveniently lists all of these agencies for you, provides their web addresses, and offers a brief summary of what they usually fund.

Read all you can find about any grants that may fit your organization. Sometimes there are multiple pages of information for potential applicants. There may be a schedule of expected deadlines. There is usually a list of previous awardees, often with the abstracts from their winning applications. The websites may provide information about upcoming workshops for grant applicants or changes to legislation you won't hear about anywhere else.

Some matches are obvious. If you provide services to support veterans, you definitely would research the Department of Veterans Affairs first. If you are in the field of health care, you would probably start with Health and Human Services and its many subagencies.

Some potential agency matches are more surprising. If you are located in a rural area or small town or if you provide services that benefit residents of rural areas, always check the US Department of Agriculture. Of course, this department funds programs and research in support of farmers and improving agriculture. But its reach extends far beyond farmers and touches housing, utilities, education, community facilities, school nutrition programs, small businesses, and more.

Under the Freedom of Information Act (FOIA), you can request copies of funded proposals. All it takes is a letter making a FOIA request for a copy of the specific proposal (for example, 2012 Appalachian State University Upward Bound). Agencies can take months to fulfill FOIA requests, and some information, such as salaries, will be redacted so you can't read it. But if you are planning ahead for the next competition, seeing how one successful applicant did it last time can give you a good model to follow.

Once you have read all you can find, make note of the program officer's name and contact information. There are lots of reasons it makes sense to contact a program officer before applying.

Contacting Program Officers

Program officers are advocates for the grant programs they oversee. Especially in these times of reduced funding, many are under increased pressure to convince the agency's leadership and Congress that their grant programs are needed and produce important results in the communities where the money is awarded. This means they want quality grantees and quality programs with strong outcomes that demonstrate success.

In short, they are the experts about the grant program. They can give you lots of valuable information. Just be sure to do your research before contacting them so you don't annoy them with simple questions that are addressed by the website's FAQ. Also, if you can contact them when there is no current deadline, they often have much more freedom to give you advice and information.

> Every funding agency is different, and every program officer is different. Some want to help you design your program before you apply and are very hands on. Other agencies seem to almost muzzle their program officers, or the program officers are nonresponsive or even give inaccurate information. Talk to a few current grantees. They can quickly let you know the culture of the agency you are interested in and the personality of the individual you need to talk to.
>
>
> important

The program officer might be able to do the following:

◆ Tell you when (or if) the funding opportunity will be available again.

◆ Give insight into the future direction of the program.

◆ Point to grantees the officer considers particularly successful.

◆ Tell you how many applicants the program usually gets or the ratio of submitted grants to those awarded.

◆ Give you feedback on your project idea.

◆ Direct you to a list of previously funded organizations.

Program officers are very busy once a deadline is approaching. Once an RFA has been released and a competition is open, they are less likely to give you any advice other than to quote the *Federal Register* or grant guidelines back to you. However, if you contact program officers between competitions, they often have great freedom to assist you.

Learning the Funder's Language Translates into a Great Relationship

Several years ago, Karen decided to contact the program officer for a Department of Education grant that looked like a good fit for the university where she worked.

But before picking up the phone, she did a quick online search. She wanted to read up on the program officer himself. Searching for congressional testimony, conference presentations, and articles unearthed some comments the program officer had made about the globalization of education and work. His personal vision for this particular grant program was to use it to help transform professions across nations and leverage shared knowledge for greater impact.

Armed with this information, Karen focused her conversation with the program officer on how her employer's new program was responsive to the globalized needs of the profession and had been designed with partners from international institutions. She painted a picture of how a grant from this program could play a pivotal role in transforming globally the profession her university wanted to target and how the shared knowledge of the partners contributed to a greater impact.

Needless to say, he was interested because she was speaking his language!

Everything she said was true. She did not change the program to fit the program officer's interests. She simply made sure to frame her project's purposes and outcomes in the program officer's language.

Basing a relationship with the program officer on solid research into his interests and submitting a solid proposal reflecting the program officer's input resulted in a $1.5 million grant to the collaborative of universities.

Search the Federal Databases

You can identify possible funding prospects by researching what grants your colleagues have won and by mining agency websites. But the list of prospects generated this way is probably incomplete. You can also use the two free federal databases of grant opportunities: the Catalog of Federal Domestic Assistance, or CFDA (cfda.gov), and Grants.gov.

Think of your searching strategy like a funnel. At the top of the funnel, the broadest portion, are keyword searches. You use these to search for any grants related to housing for seniors or domestic violence.

A bit narrower is searching by the funding agency. If you know that the Office on Violence Against Women provides the most funding opportunities related to domestic violence, you can search on that agency.

More specific is the name of a particular funding program. Upward Bound for education, or Safe Havens for domestic violence.

Finally, the most specific of all is searching by the Funding Opportunity Number or CFDA number. If you have one of these numbers, you can zoom directly to the specific grant opportunity you are interested in.

But let's start at the broad end of the funnel first.

Searching on Key Words or Terms

It's great to have some specific programs narrowed down to research further. However, if you want to do exploratory searching to find out what other grants might be out there, turn to the databases.

In our experience, the CFDA does a better job of returning results relevant to key words than does Grants.gov. There are a few reasons for this, but one way to close the gap is to make sure when searching Grants.gov to check the "archived" and "closed" boxes along with the default "open" box before hitting "search."

Including Closed and Archived Opportunities

One of the frustrating things about Grants.gov is its default to show you only currently open

> Keep this distinction between Grants.gov and CFDA in mind—grant opportunities versus grant programs.
>
> ◆ Grants.gov is a listing of grant applications. Its default is to show only currently open applications. Once a deadline has passed, the application is off the list unless you proactively select the ability to search closed and archived opportunities.
>
> ◆ CFDA is a listing of grant programs. Programs don't appear then drop off the list based on deadlines but stay pretty consistent. Some programs may have multiple applications (meaning that one CFDA program may generate multiple Grants.gov applications).
>
>

grant opportunities. If you search for domestic violence funding opportunities in September and all of the Office on Violence Against Women opportunities had deadlines in April, you will get no results from this funder.

So it's usually best to check the "closed" and "archived" boxes on the search screen every time. Unfortunately, when we searched Grants.gov for open, closed, and archived opportunities with our search terms "domestic violence" in quotation marks, up popped almost 1,500 grant titles to slog through. Some make sense: "Grants to Reduce Sexual Assault, Domestic Violence, Dating Violence, and Stalking on Campus." Others just make you laugh: "Water Conservation Field Services Program." It almost makes you want to go read that one to see just how they weave domestic violence issues into water conservation programs.

Fortunately, there are a few strategies for narrowing your search results. For example, you can ask Grants.gov to show results only from certain agencies. In the domestic violence example, many of those 1,500 results were for international programs (protecting women in Iraq or Sudan). You could check lots of agency boxes on the Grants.gov screen but leave USAID unchecked, and that would immediately shorten the list.

When searching for a term such as "domestic violence," putting both words into quotation marks will yield results with these two words together, in this order. If you search for domestic violence without question marks, the search will return results of all occurrences of the word "domestic" and all occurrences of the word "violence," whether they are together or not.

CFDA versus Grants.gov

Conducting the same search on CFDA for "domestic violence" with quotation marks around the terms yields 39 results instead of almost 1,500. The first 20 of these results are all from the Office on Violence Against Women. The second half mostly all make sense and come from other parts of the Department of Justice or Health and Human Services.

The other nice feature of CFDA searches is that you can use a check box to select the grant programs you are interested in and export the list to Excel.

Searching by Agency

Both Grants.gov and CFDA have powerful advanced searching features that allow you to apply all sorts of criteria to your searching. Applying more criteria returns a shorter list, but if you are careful, the list can be more accurate.

Both sites allow you to limit your search to only selected agencies. In some instances, this can help narrow your search results tremendously. In other cases, such as asking to see all open, closed, and archived opportunities from the Department of Education, Grants.gov returns more than 650 results. You have no option to narrow the types of grants to K–12 or postsecondary education. In contrast, CFDA allows you to choose from among the Department of Education's 12 suboffices. This is why we recommend you reproduce your searches on both sites.

Searching by Grant Name or CFDA Number

The strategies of searching by keyword/topic or funding agency are methods you use when you want to build a list of possible funding opportunities to pursue. However, when you need information on a specific grant, you want to zero in on that grant as quickly as possible so you can read the profile or access the funding announcement.

Always note the Funding Opportunity Number or Catalog of Federal Domestic Assistance (CFDA) number for any grant opportunity you are interested in. Those numbers are the quickest, most accurate way to access a specific funding opportunity in Grants.gov so you can get the guidelines.

If you know the name of a grant opportunity, such as "Upward Bound" or "Safe Havens," you can enter that name as your keyword search. This will usually return accurate results on either site. (Don't forget the quotation marks, and don't forget to include "closed, archived, and open" on Grants.gov.)

Finally, having the CFDA number for a grant opportunity is the most precise method of searching. It still may return two or three application options that are variations of the same program, but you will get the summary and guidelines for that particular program only.

Registering for Grant Email Alerts

You can supplement active searching with receiving daily email alerts from Grants.gov or the *Federal Register*. These alerts let you know whenever an RFA has been released and a deadline is open. They are short and clearly marked by funding agency and grant title. These announcements are a great way to make sure you don't miss any opportunities you may not have turned up in your research. We also find them very useful even when we know about the program, because we are usually waiting for the guidelines to come out and for the deadline to be announced.

Paid Subscription Services

Doing your own research is smart and will teach you quite a lot about what funding opportunities you can expect to be available to you over the next few years. But we like to supplement our research and our email alerts with information from paid subscription services.

> Don't depend solely on the email alerts. They are sent when the funding opportunity opens. This usually leaves you with little time to pull together a proposal with all of the forms, narratives, and attachments. Even experienced applicants will admit that putting together a competitive application in a short period of time is stressful.

 practical tip

In our opinion, it's worth paying the fee only if the service does more for you than just regurgitate the Grants.gov or *Federal Register* email alerts. Find a service that predicts which grants are likely to be announced and gives you other important information, such as which funding programs will have reduced funding or which may get increases. Also, consider a service with contacts at the agencies in which you are interested. Such services invest time and energy in tracking legislation, regulations, and the seemingly never-ending budget uncertainties to keep you up to date on the funding landscape.

Some services are industry specific and focus on certain issues, such as tribal funding or HUD projects. Others are broader. Some services come as part of your dues to another organization and may include some state grant announcements as well.

How to Get an RFA

Whether you access information about a grant through Grants.gov or CFDA, once you click on the name of a funding opportunity or program, you will see a summary of the program's most pertinent information. It can be useful to access the summary on both sites, because they prioritize different information.

Writing to Win Federal Grants–The Workbook includes an entire CFDA listing that is annotated to guide you through its various elements and show you how to use these to supplement your Grants.gov research.

The Workbook

On the CFDA site, you usually see contact information for a program officer highlighted right at the top of the screen, but information about deadlines can be limited. The Grants.gov website shows you the next upcoming deadline—or the most recent one if the competition is not currently open. It also usually has the most current information about who is eligible to apply and the anticipated number of awards.

Below is a screen shot of how Grants.gov looked when this book went to press. Despite small design changes from time to time, the most basic content remains the same.

Notice the name of the grant program is in big type under the words "view grant opportunity." Beneath those words, the white tab tells you that you are on the synopsis page.

In the left column are the funding opportunity number, the expected number of awards, and the CFDA number. It also says that matching funds are required for this grant. The right column lists the closing date (deadline), the award ceiling (the maximum grant allowed), and the award floor (the minimum grant allowed).

CONTACT US | MANAGE SUBSCRIPTIONS | REGISTER | LOGIN

GRANTS.GOV℠

FIND. APPLY. SUCCEED.℠

SEARCH: Grant Opportunities ⌄   Enter Keyword...   GO

HOME   ABOUT ⌄   SEARCH GRANTS ⌄   APPLICANTS ⌄   GRANTORS ⌄   SYSTEM-TO-SYSTEM ⌄   FORMS ⌄   OUTREACH ⌄   SUPPORT ⌄

GRANTS.GOV 〉 *Search Grants*

VIEW GRANT OPPORTUNITY

‹ Back | Link

L21-FY14
Laura Bush 21st Century Librarian Program
Institute of Museum and Library Services

| SYNOPSIS DETAILS | VERSION HISTORY | FULL ANNOUNCEMENT | APPLICATION PACKAGE |

The synopsis for this grant opportunity is detailed below, following this paragraph. This synopsis contains all of the updates to this document that have been posted as of 7/22/2013. If updates have been made to the opportunity synopsis, update information is provided below the synopsis.

If you would like to receive notifications of changes to the grant opportunity click send me change notification emails. The only thing you need to provide for this service is your email address. No other information is requested.

Any inconsistency between the original printed document and the disk or electronic document shall be resolved by giving precedence to the printed document

General Information

Document Type:	Grants Notice	Posted Date:	Jul 22, 2013
Funding Opportunity Number:	L21-FY14	Creation Date:	Jul 22, 2013
Funding Opportunity Title:	Laura Bush 21st Century Librarian Program	Original Closing Date for Applications:	Sep 16, 2013
Opportunity Category:	Discretionary	Current Closing Date for Applications:	Sep 16, 2013
Funding Instrument Type:	Grant	Archive Date:	Oct 16, 2013
Category of Funding Activity:	Arts (see "Cultural Affairs" in CFDA) Humanities (see "Cultural Affairs" in CFDA)	Estimated Total Program Funding:	$12,000,000
		Award Ceiling:	$500,000
Category Explanation:		Award Floor:	$50,000
Expected Number of Awards:	40		
CFDA Number(s):	45.313 – Laura Bush 21st Century Librarian Program		
Cost Sharing or Matching Requirement:	Yes		

Clicking on the "full announcement" and "application package" tabs will allow you to access even more information. This screen shot shows only the top half of the results screen, but it includes the most important information.

If the information on the summary page still looks like a good fit, it's time to go get the entire RFA. Seems easy enough, since Grants.gov provides you with a handy "full announcement" tab at the top of the screen. Sigh. Sometimes you strike gold. But nothing is wrong with your web browser if this page comes up completely blank. If nothing appears here, try these steps:

◆ Go back to the summary page (currently called "synopsis details") and see if there is a link close to the bottom of the page next to the "Additional Information" heading.

◆ Click on the "Application Package" tab at the top of the screen, click through a few more steps, and make sure to download both the application instructions and the application package when you finally get the chance.

◆ With CFDA number in hand, go straight to the agency's website and search its grants pages for guidelines.

Don't forget that not all grants can be submitted through Grants.gov. Even if you find a synopsis of the funding opportunity at Grants.gov, you may need to go to the agency's website to get the RFA or to access an alternate submission system.

important

Be aware that the application package is something completely different from the guidelines. If the agency is using Grants.gov for submittal, you must download the application package from Grants.gov regardless of where the guidelines are published. The package is a large PDF file. It has fillable fields, places to attach your narratives and other attachments, and forms to complete. It may have the instructions for completing forms, but it does not contain the guidelines for the particular grant for which you are applying.

Sometimes it feels as if successfully obtaining the RFA is the first step in the agency's weeding-out process. If you can unravel the mystery of finding the grant guidelines, you've passed the first hurdle. The next chapter gives you a road map for skimming an RFA to determine quickly whether the opportunity is a good fit for your organization.

Writing to Win Federal Grants–The Workbook contains a worksheet to help you organize your research and keep track of what opportunities will come open when.

The
Workbook

Once you have gathered all of this information on programs to which you want to apply over the next year, it's a good idea to develop a system for organizing the information electronically or in notebooks. A simple Word or Excel document can help you keep potential funding opportunities organized. If you still prefer hard-copy records or like to keep them as a backup, three-ring binders organized by topic are an effective way to organize your grant opportunities.

To Recap

◆ Free online services like the CFDA and Grants.gov make finding potential good-fit opportunities accessible to all, while paid subscriptions can be a valuable addition to your research.

◆ Searching closed and archived funding opportunities will help you identify the full range of funding opportunities and programs that can support your organization's work.

◆ Taking the time to learn as much as possible about program officers and then talking to them between application cycles can build strong relationships.

◆ Use the summary on a grant's synopsis page to determine if you need to access the RFA for more information.

Chapter Five

Deciding When to Go for It: Assessing an RFA

IN THIS CHAPTER

    ···→ Winnowing down the list of possible prospects identified by your research

    ···→ Encountering an RFA for the first time—how not to get overwhelmed

    ···→ Using an objective checklist to make a go/no-go decision

    ···→ Reading for detail once you've found "the one"

You've followed our research tips, and now you have a list of potential prospects. With grant programs sometimes having confusing titles or searches turning up dozens of results, you will have to kiss a lot of frogs before you find one that's a good match. (Okay, you may find two, but two federal proposals are a lot to handle if they are your first, so try to limit yourself to one at a time when it comes time to actually apply.)

Then you click to read the guidelines for a program at the top of your list to find out if you are a match. Yikes, are they long!

Grants colleagues often tell us that they are very confident in their ability to win foundation grants but that federal guidelines make them want to run the other way. We understand. The guidelines for how to apply can run eighty pages or longer. Sometimes the guidelines are spread around multiple documents that you have to gather together yourself.

Don't let the RFA intimidate you. When it comes time to read the whole thing, we will offer several tips to help you slog through what can look kind of scary the first time you see it. But that's not where you start.

You are not a failure if you find only a few grants for which you are eligible. Especially if this is your first federal grant, be patient and take the time to find one that's best suited to your organization. It's okay to reject several opportunities as not being the right type of program or not coming at the right time for your organization.

The first time you encounter an RFA, you are trying only to determine if this may be "the one." We call this making a go/no-go decision. Fortunately, you have our prioritized RFA decision points below, a magic wand that helps you weed out the frogs pretty quickly. If the decision is to not apply, you can ignore the rest of the RFA.

Try to think of your first encounter with an RFA as speed dating. You want just the highlights. After you've culled your one or two top prospects from the herd, that's when you get serious. Then you're digging in for the whole life story, deciding if this is someone you can spend the rest of your life with. Thankfully, you don't have to get that deep with most RFAs because you will reject them pretty early on.

Skimming the RFA for Highlights

We can't tell you how many times we've been lured in by a pretty profile on a grant's summary page only to find out we aren't eligible to apply or we can't meet an important requirement. This is why we recommend jumping to some important sections in the RFA first rather than starting to read right at the beginning.

The beginning of the RFA is usually the feel-good stuff about why this grant exists, who it is designed to serve, and what sort of services it will fund. It is easy to read those first several pages and get excited about how this is the perfect grant for your organization.

But resist the urge. First, skim for key information in the order presented in the list below. It will save you hours of time. It is discouraging to read pages and pages of an RFA, getting

excited about how much your organization can accomplish with the grant funds, only to find out after reading twenty-five or thirty pages that you are not eligible or that it would not be a good decision to apply at this particular time.

Almost every one of the items on the following list can be a decision point. You want to know right away if this is an opportunity you have to say no to before you invest too much time and energy in planning a project. Many organizations have a go/no-go process for every grant opportunity. A checklist in **Appendix G** summarizes the information on the next page

Usually, important information about the grant—such as funding amounts, deadline, and who is eligible to apply—appears on the announcement page on Grants.gov. Start there. If that information sounds promising, download the RFA to dig more deeply. Use the RFA decision points provided in this chapter or the checklist in **Appendix G** to hit the most important details first.

and provides you with a way to keep an organized record of each grant opportunity, whether you decided to pursue the opportunity, and why that decision was made. It even includes a place for an approval signature. This checklist comes from *Writing to Win Federal Grants–The Workbook*, which contains many more such tools.

Prioritized RFA Decision Points

1. *Purpose.* Carefully read the funding agency's stated purpose for providing grant funding. It is essential that there be a close match between what the grant will fund and your existing mission. If there is no mission fit, reject the RFA immediately.

2. *Eligibility.* Next, skip to what types of applicants are allowed. You may be knocked out of the competition right at this stage. For instance, some competitions are open only to nonprofits with 501(c)(3) status, while others are open only to state or local governmental agencies. Some are open to nonprofits who have not yet received their 501(c)(3) status, and some are even open to for-profits.

3. *Deadline.* How much time do you have to pull this application together? Can it realistically be done, given your other duties and the level of detail needed in the program design? Is it a ten-page narrative or a fifty-page narrative? If your organization is not already registered in Grants.gov and SAM (see **Appendix C**), that will add to your time crunch.

4. *Funding amounts.* Check both the funding "ceiling" and the "floor." A "floor" is the minimum amount you are allowed to ask for in the grant budget. Yes, there really are minimum grant amounts. Of course, the ceiling is the maximum amount you are allowed to request. Since your application will be rejected if you submit a budget that is less than the floor or exceeds the ceiling, you must realistically assess whether you can implement your planned program with the amount of funding available.

   Also consider the size of the grant award relative to your organization's budget. Reviewers and the funding agency often consider whether your grant request is proportional to an organization's size. Too dramatic a change too quickly can overwhelm your organization. The funding agency may also have concerns

> *Matching funds:* Some federal programs require that applicants match any amount provided through the grant. The rules for how the match is calculated, what you are allowed to count as a match, and when you must have the match (or a pledge) secured vary significantly from program to program, so read carefully.
>
> *In-kind contributions:* Tangible things your organization (or partners) contributes to a grant-funded program that are not charged to the grant, such as office space, furniture, office equipment, personnel, and so on.
>
>

about your ability to manage a large grant. An organization with an annual budget of $2 million is more likely to successfully operate a $300,000-per-year program than an organization that has never managed more than $75,000 a year. Is the grant you are considering a reasonable size for your organization to handle?

5. *Matching requirements.* Are matching funds required? In what ratio? Is the match required to be all cash, or are you allowed to count in-kind contributions toward the match? Some organizations are unable to raise the funds required for a cash match. If so, they should not pursue the current opportunity under consideration.

6. *Anticipated number of awards.* This number gives you a hint about how competitive the program is. If more than fifty awards are going to be made, you can hope for at least one per state. If fewer than ten awards are going to be made, competition for this opportunity will be incredibly tough. You may decide to pass unless you know you are extremely competitive for a particular reason. If only one or two awards will be made, they will probably go to applicants with preexisting relationships with the funding agency.

Memorandum of Understanding (MOU) or *Memorandum of Agreement* (MOA): A formal written agreement between partners in a project; sometimes required by federal agencies.

 finition

---

7. *Partnering requirements.* Are you required to have formal partners or a coalition to apply? How formal? Do you have time to develop the necessary relationships or to obtain a signed Memorandum of Understanding?

8. *Level of evaluation required.* What sort of evaluation effort does this application require? Are you expected to hire an external evaluator? Do you have the resources and expertise necessary (or can you obtain them) to conduct an evaluation of the sort the funding agency expects? Evaluation requirements can make or break a project plan, so consider them carefully.

9. *Regular competition or one-time chance.* Many programs are ongoing, with regular competitions annually or every two to four years. Other grants are one-time only. Will you get another chance to respond if you must decline this time?

10. *Technical assistance.* Will there be a workshop or webinar offered by the agency to help applicants apply? Often these are scheduled very soon after the RFA is released, so be sure to search the document for "technical assistance," "conference call," and "webinar" as soon as you get the RFA. You don't want to miss any workshops.

11. *Extra points.* Find out if extra points are awarded for prior experience (current recipients of the grant you are applying for) or for items labeled "Competitive Preference Priorities" or "Bonus Points." Some programs are so competitive that if

you are not able to earn prior experience points, you are often advised not to even bother applying. If there are points awarded for other priorities, consider if you can meet those priorities. You will need every point you can get.

Deciding Not to Apply

Don't be afraid to decide not to apply for a grant. Federal grant applications require an enormous investment of time, usually from several people within your organization. As the grant professional, you are the expert on the funding opportunity. It is your job to be prepared to make a recommendation of "go" or "no go" on an application.

Use the RFA decision points and checklist in **Appendix G** to carefully analyze funding opportunities. The visual reinforcement of lots of checks in the yes or no columns can help back up your recommendation regarding whether or not to pursue this grant.

Now that most RFAs come out in electronic format, using your word processor or PDF reader's word search function can help you find references to things such as technical assistance workshops, page limits, margin requirements, and other important details.

Deciding to Go for It

If the funding opportunity passes the RFA checklist test and you've made the decision that this is "the one," get out your highlighter. We've put it off as long as possible. Now it's time to dive in. Read the entire RFA carefully, watching for important details that can be sprinkled in unpredictable places throughout the document.

The good news is that most RFAs from the same funding agency follow a predictable format. You will learn their style with a little practice. For example, some RFAs include lengthy instructions on how to register on Grants.gov and/or get your DUNS number. You have to do this only once.

Read a print version of the RFA with highlighters and sticky notes in hand to mark important details, such as spacing requirements or required attachments. Use the highlighting or comments feature of your word processing or PDF software to do the same if you are reading an electronic RFA.

Some RFAs look artificially long because entire pages of content are included twice. Other agencies place standard "how to write an application" text in all of their funding announcements. Once you see this content a few times, you will recognize it and know to set it aside until you are creating your writing outline.

The good news is you will find that you are already familiar with much of the content because you have already reviewed it when making your decision whether to respond.

Do Page Limits Really Count?

Yes, they do! An organization recently told us they thought page limits were just a suggestion. No, no, no.

A proposal Cheryl worked on was once rejected for going one page over the page limit. It was a mistake. A table of contents was added by another person at the last minute, and the table of contents counted against the page limit. Normally, adding a page to the beginning of a document would renumber the subsequent pages so that it would be clear by looking at the last page that the document was suddenly one page too long.

But, for reasons too complicated to explain here, Cheryl had inserted a section break in the middle of the document and manually forced the page numbering to begin again at page 21 after the break. Ten pages could have been added to the beginning of that document, and the page number on the last page would not have changed. Anyone checking the page number on the last page would think the narrative was still within the limits. The grant had to be submitted without Cheryl reviewing it one final time, so no one realized it was one page too long.

The funding agency would not score the proposal because it was not compliant with the guidelines. Lots of strange things can happen to your automatically numbered pages. That's why we recommend either scrolling through or printing out every single page and checking the page number on every page right before submitting.

stories from the real world

But don't get careless. Read the entire thing. It's not unusual for RFAs to include errors or even contradict themselves. In the case of an outright contradiction (such as the number of pages allowed or an allowable expense), contact the program officer and get written clarification. Never guess.

Aside from getting to know the entire document more intimately than you know your best friend, some key highlights to be noting as you read include:

◆ *Allowable activities.* Which types of activities can you undertake, and which are prohibited? For example, the Department of Health and Human Services funds capacity-building grants for rural health care networks. Under that specific funding opportunity, grant recipients are not allowed to deliver health services with grant funds. Funds may be used only to develop the network's operations, such as through professional development, consulting, or developing a business plan.

◆ *Allowable expenses.* What things or services are you allowed to spend grant funds on? Sometimes allowable expenses and allowable activities are not exactly the same. You may be allowed to conduct a particular activity but be expected to use matching funds or other organizational resources to do so and are not allowed to use grant funds. For example, your project may call for delivering health education classes, and you may be renovating space for a classroom. If construction costs are not an allowable expense, your organization would be expected to renovate the classroom using other funds but could request all other expenses for delivering the program in the grant budget.

◆ *Deadline date and time.* Sometimes we write in really big letters right on the front of print RFAs, or enter into our calendars, the deadline date and time in *our* time zone. Some grants are due by 4:30 p.m. Eastern time. If you forget and submit at 4:30 p.m. in your time zone, your application will be late. We always recommend submitting a few days ahead of the deadline, but we've all had last-minute emergencies.

> Make a cheat sheet for tracking important information like deadline date, deadline time, formatting requirements, page limits, how and in what order documents are to be uploaded, etc. Federal agencies receive thousands of applications and make grant awards to only a small percentage of applicants. Failing to follow instructions to the last detail can result in your proposal being rejected without ever being reviewed.

practical tip

◆ *Priorities.* Sometimes extra points are available if your project meets certain priorities, such as being able to prove that your organization is in a rural location. Sometimes no extra points are available but the RFA says that a type of activity will receive priority consideration, such as whether your program to serve at-risk high school students includes outreach to homeless students. It's good to know about any such priorities before designing your program so you can tweak the program if necessary to incorporate any priorities that you can. Of course, you can't change your location, but if adding outreach to homeless youth does not conflict with your program's mission, consider adding it to get the points. Just be sure to think of any possible budget implications.

◆ *Data needs.* Make a list of all the data you will need to support your case for need or to prove that your project design is based on previous successes (sometimes called "evidence-based"). At larger organizations, you may need to send a data request to the database person. Organizations of all sizes often need to dig into Census or other data. Consider putting someone on data collection at the very beginning of the project planning process.

◆ *Signatures required.* Find out what forms or other documents might need to be signed by someone higher up. You can begin circulating those documents for approvals while you are developing your proposal.

Armed with the most important information from the RFA and with a very clear understanding of just what the funding agency wants to support, you are ready to design a program to take to the funder.

To Recap

◆ Although your initial research may yield several possible prospects, once you dig down into the guidelines, your realistic prospect list is usually much shorter.

◆ Make your decision whether to apply based on facts and careful consideration. A checklist of important items to consider can help.

◆ It's perfectly acceptable, and indeed is usually wise, to reject a funding opportunity if it's not a good match for your organization.

◆ Once you have decided to apply, get to know your RFA by reading carefully and noting important details.

Chapter Six

Mapping Out Your Journey: Logic Models

IN THIS CHAPTER

---+ Fill-in-the-box method of project planning

---+ Essential program elements become a logic model

---+ Logic models are a road map for reviewers

Before you can start writing, you have to have something to write about. For a federal grant, that's your project or your program. We're using both of those terms to encompass whatever it is you plan on doing with the grant funds.

If your grants dream team has not already been involved, it's time to call a huddle. You may have some great project ideas, but now your team will adjust them so they fit within the parameters of the grant guidelines.

You may have a program in place that you are expanding with grant funds. Or you may need a program to serve runaway youth, but the funds have not been there. Either way, it is helpful to everyone involved to map out a clear plan for program delivery that fits the requirements of the grant you are applying for.

In the grants world, that map is often called a "logic model." It may have a weird name, but a logic model simply condenses your major program elements and communicates briefly what it will take you pages of narrative to write out in detail. A logic model can also be a powerful program planning tool.

Reading a Logic Model

Logic models appear in different formats, but one traditional design used by many funders and grant seekers organizes five boxes side by side. They are labeled "Inputs/Resources," "Activities," "Outputs," "Outcomes," and "Impact." One way to explain the relationship among each of the boxes is to think in a series of "if-then" statements. Such as, "If I had these inputs, then I could conduct these activities," and so on. Once a program diagram is complete, you read it left to right, filling in those "if-then" statements as illustrated in the diagram below:

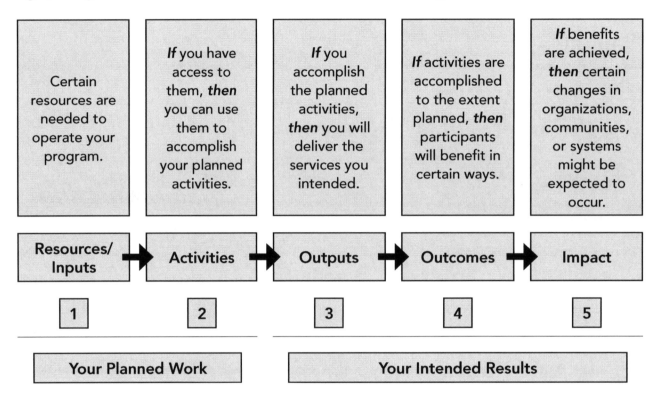

This way of explaining and reading a logic model was taken from the Kellogg Foundation and its free guide to developing logic models, available at wkkf.org.

Beginning with the End in Mind

Although we read a completed logic model from left to right, when designing a program, many people prefer to start with the ultimate goal or impact and work their way left. We have found in multiple group exercises that people often learn these elements more quickly if they can practice completing a program diagram for a nonthreatening topic completely unrelated to their organization. For example, your team may brainstorm the content of a diagram illustrating a project to "build a road linking rural Nigerian farmers to an urban area."

Logframe: Short for "Logical Framework Approach." International organizations typically use this term to refer to diagrams that we call logic models.

(de)finition

Impact

Think of impact as the long-term change expected to occur or that you hope to occur several years from now as a result of your wonderful grant project. Always think in terms of change. What will increase or decrease or improve? If you make yourself use verbs, you will be more likely to be stating an actual impact.

If you put the Nigerian road project in front of a group of your coworkers and ask them what the purpose is, most understand right away that building the road is not the purpose behind the project.

If you build a road and suddenly impoverished Nigerian farmers have a way to get their products to market in urban centers, what might change in the lives of these farmers? Brainstorm.

Increased financial stability. Improved nutrition (for the farmers and city dwellers). Better economic opportunities. If this were replicated all over the country, maybe even a stronger Nigeria.

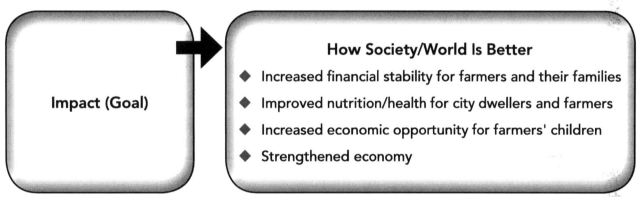

Outcomes

Outcomes describe the benefits to people served by your project or a change that takes place. Changes can take place within an organization, which can become stronger or more financially stable. Changes can affect a society or community. Or they can take place in individuals.

What kinds of things change in people or communities?

◆ Behaviors

◆ Skills

◆ Knowledge

◆ Attitudes

◆ Conditions (financial, health, economic, environmental, etc.)

KSAs: A commonly used acronym for knowledge, skills, and abilities.

d📖finition

Outcomes are what happen as a result of our activities. What has changed in a person or in our community? Does a person gain increased knowledge, skills, and abilities (KSAs)? More importantly, does a person take action as a result of learning something new?

Outcomes measure results, not activities:

◆ Reduced carbon emissions

◆ Community better equipped to respond to emergencies

◆ Healthier homebound population

◆ Reduced groundwater pollution

The types of outcomes you list in your logic model depend on what you want to achieve with your program. If you were brainstorming logical outcomes of your road-building project in Nigeria, what do you suppose some of them would be? What sorts of outcomes would you have to produce to reach your projected impacts?

Outcomes

What Happens in the Community

◆ Increased sales for farmers

◆ Reduced waste from spoilage

◆ Increased access to healthy food for city residents

◆ Increased sales opportunities for city vendors to farmers

◆ Farmers' families able to purchase more food

◆ Farmers' families able to afford education

Outputs

Usually, if you can count something, it is an output, not an outcome. How many classes were taught? How many individuals were screened for diabetes? How many miles of road were constructed? Outputs are "widgets." They are the "things" that a project produces:

◆ Number of people served, trained, fed, housed

◆ Number of classes offered

◆ Number of website hits or ads placed

◆ Number of units rehabbed

Outputs are great. They are essential to our projects. We must measure them to make sure we are meeting our objectives. The problem is, outputs have little value unless achieving them leads to a desired outcome or impact.

To keep this straight, here is an outputs versus outcomes cheat sheet:

Outputs	Outcomes
◆ Things we can count, "widgets"	◆ Things we can measure, change
◆ Shorter term	◆ End of project period
◆ Process:	◆ Results:
❖ Two buildings retrofitted	❖ Utility usage reduced
❖ Twenty-five meals delivered	❖ Health improves

Just keep saying to yourself "change, change, change" when you are asked to talk about outcomes. Your outputs are important and should lead logically into your outcomes. It is not enough to create exceptional outcomes if readers cannot see a clear path from your outputs to the outcomes. For our hypothetical Nigerian road project, what might the project outputs be?

Well, it seems like the most important thing to measure is that the road was completed. You should probably measure how many miles were built. For such a simple project, it might be sufficient to stop with just one output. However, we propose a few more that might be reasonable and might even be expected by a funder who supports road-building projects as a way to achieve economic development.

Beware of being too insular when thinking of desired outputs. For example, a common mistake is to list something like "new program manager hired" as an output or outcome of a grant project. Hiring a person is just a means to an end. Why are you hiring that person? So that fifty students may be served? So that your clinic expands its hours? The answer to the "why" question represents your true result.

Outputs

◆ 25 miles of road built

◆ 250 locals employed

◆ 5 local suppliers used

◆ 150 people used the road within 30 days of its opening

Activities

Activities are the meat of your program. They are what your program does. Activities use the resources that you determine are needed (inputs) so that you can achieve the desired outputs and outcomes. Activities are defined by action verbs. Someone is doing something to or for someone else.

Typical grant program activities include the following:

◆ Building/renovating something

◆ Teaching classes/workshops

◆ Hiring someone

◆ Conducting marketing campaigns

◆ Developing something (curriculum, new service)

◆ Counseling/treating/educating people

The list can go on and on. Of course, all of these tasks can be broken down into multiple subtasks. In order to build something, you must complete multiple tasks along the way, including planning, getting bids, selecting contractors, and the like.

Now turn your mind back to that road project in Nigeria. Notice that we said only that you were building a road. We did not say what type of road or what materials you have to use. As a result, when we give this activity to groups, we get many, many different road designs.

If you are the organization directing the project, your activities list may look like the following:

If you are the contractor building the road, your activities list may look more like this:

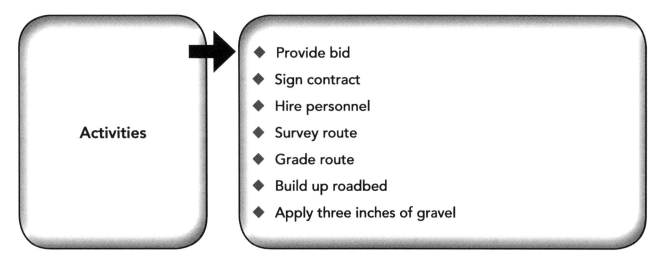

Activities

- Provide bid
- Sign contract
- Hire personnel
- Survey route
- Grade route
- Build up roadbed
- Apply three inches of gravel

Limit the activities listed in your program diagram to only those that can be completed within the scope and timeline of the grant project. Maybe you have to develop curriculum before you can teach a class. But if the grant covers only teaching and not course development, then find a way to indicate activities that must take place preaward, or on your own time, and distinguish them from grant-funded tasks.

Inputs

"Inputs" is just a jargon term for "resources." What resources will it take for you to implement the project you are proposing? The most obvious one is money. You need the grant to do the project, or you wouldn't be writing this proposal.

In addition, what other resources will the grant money help you obtain? These are resources that you absolutely have to have to deliver your project. You can also list resources that you will bring to the table to supplement the grant. This is most important if you are required to match grant funds or otherwise demonstrate organizational commitment to the project.

Typical inputs include the following:

- Money
- Staff
- Volunteers
- Facilities/space
- Equipment
- Supplies
- Expertise

Do those bullets ring any bells for you? What about the federal budget categories? Yes, inputs are what you are going to spend your grant money on. In this way, the logic model actually helps you make your case for your budget because it is directly tied to your budget. The logic model helps readers see immediately how your grant funds will be spent.

The type of inputs for your project depends on many variables. In some projects, your organization's clients or consumers of your services are necessary inputs. In others, matching funds, partner contributions, or other types of in-kind support may be inputs.

The items in the list above are only categories. If you have extremely limited space, you could get away with limiting yourself to stating your inputs in that way. However, if you have more room, it's best to get more specific.

Returning to the Nigerian road-building project, try to brainstorm some inputs that are more specific than "supplies." Since you are probably not a roads expert, and this is just an exercise, feel free to make up your inputs. The practice should still help you identify inputs for your own program.

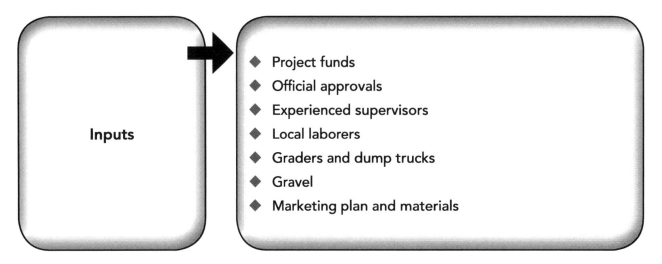

Inputs

◆ Project funds
◆ Official approvals
◆ Experienced supervisors
◆ Local laborers
◆ Graders and dump trucks
◆ Gravel
◆ Marketing plan and materials

Pulling It All Together

Once you have completed each of the pieces of the program diagram, you can compose the completed matrix. Ours from the Nigerian road-building project will look something like the one illustrated on the next page.

Reading Like a Reviewer

Grant reviewers sometimes pull out an application's logic model and program budget and read those before reading the longer narrative. The logic model helps give them an overview of the project being proposed.

On page 56 is a logic model from a federal proposal to the Department of Education. The program being funded was a capacity-building program. This means that funds could not be used to serve students, only to strengthen the institution so that it would be better able to serve students. An important distinction.

Logic Model Illustration of Nigerian Road-Building Project

Inputs	Activities	Outputs	Outcomes	Impacts
◆ Project funds ◆ Official approvals ◆ Experienced supervisors ◆ Local laborers ◆ Graders and dump trucks ◆ Gravel ◆ Marketing plan and materials	◆ Approve design ◆ Request and vet bids ◆ Sign contract ◆ Supervise contractors ◆ Celebrate completion ◆ Marketing to inform community of road's availability	◆ 25 miles of road built ◆ 250 locals employed ◆ 5 local suppliers used ◆ 150 people use the road within 30 days of opening	◆ Increased sales for farmers ◆ Reduced food waste due to spoilage ◆ Increased healthy food for city residents ◆ Increased sales for city vendors to farmers ◆ Farmers' families able to purchase more food ◆ Farmers' families able to afford education	◆ Increased financial stability for farmers and their families ◆ Improved nutrition/ health for city dwellers and farmers ◆ Increased economic opportunity for farmer's children ◆ Strengthened economy

Just by reviewing the one-page snapshot of the program on the next page, you can get a good idea of its major components. These should also give you clues to look for parallels in the budget. You may not know what an ILS is (any abbreviations and acronyms were spelled out numerous times in the project narrative so that readers were familiar with them), but you won't be surprised to see a large amount of money set aside to purchase one—based on this diagram.

We allowed ourselves to use abbreviations and even symbols because we had extremely limited space. We chose to list as inputs items that had big line items associated with them in the budget to help readers see their value and role in the project. Also, the bigger the budget item, the easier it is to attach outcomes to it.

Another way to interpret the following example is that the "Inputs" column can support the need statement. Your planned grant activities need

> Your logic model will change, probably more than once. The planning process is iterative. You need the plans to begin writing. But usually the process of writing uncovers flaws in the program plan or identifies missing pieces that you need to go back and add. The program diagram is a guide, not the law.
>
>
> important

to demonstrate they have a direct connection with the needs or problems that you will identify in the need statement of the project narrative. Notice that the first input, "Faculty with new skill sets," leads directly to a logical grant activity, "Provide faculty development." We have the faculty. But for them to do what we need them to accomplish with this grant, they need beefed-up skills.

EXCERPT...

Logic Model—Kellogg Program Implementation Style

Inputs	Activities	Outputs	Outcomes	Impact
To accomplish our activities, we will need the following:	To address our weaknesses we will accomplish these activities:	Accomplished activities will produce this evidence:	Accomplished activities will lead to these changes:	Accomplished activities will lead to long-term changes:
- Faculty with new skill sets	- Provide faculty development	- Number of faculty trained	- Increased use of active learning	- Improved Retention
- *New curriculum for Learning Communities*	- *Design new courses*	- *# of courses developed*	- *More students persist*	- Improved Six-Year Graduation Rates
- Adequate access to library resources	- Obtain ILS and enter LC info	- More faculty & students use library resources	- Improved learning; better papers	- Increased Enrollment
- *Trained pool of student tutors*	- *Develop SI program*	- *Number of tutors hired & trained*	- *Better grades*	- Stronger Institution
- Complete, accurate student data	- Build systems and skills to collect & track data	- Data is being collected, tracked and analyzed	- Decisions and plans are data driven	- Improved Fiscal Position
- *Start-up funding*	- *Title III grant*	- *Funds received*	- *Univ. financially strengthened*	
- Personnel focused on project activities	- Release/hire staff; assign responsibilities	- Project activities being completed	- Improved student services	

Writing to Win Federal Grants–The Workbook includes several sample logic models you can adapt for your own use. It also provides tools you can use to guide project design discussions with program staff and teach them about project elements in a nonthreatening exercise.

The Workbook

While many logic models follow the left-to-right columnar format we have demonstrated in this chapter, they can take many different forms and sizes. They can easily be adjusted to reflect more complex projects or simpler project designs. You can also use the boxes of a logic model to teach others at your organization about project design from the grantor's perspective. **Appendix K** includes links to free online resources for learning more about logic models and even an online logic model builder.

Now that you have some basic bullets for your project, it's time to put some budget numbers on those bullets.

To Recap

◆ Good program diagrams help tell the story of your project and make clear linkages from your planned activities to your proposed outcomes.

◆ Reviewers sometimes read logic models and budgets first to get a snapshot of your proposal.

◆ The logic model can help justify major budget expenditures.

Chapter Seven

Budgets and Budget Narratives

IN THIS CHAPTER

···→ Using the budget to tell your grant's story

···→ Organizing expenses in federal budget categories

···→ Explaining expenses in the budget narrative

···→ Direct and indirect costs

Wait! We are talking budget before we even start writing? Absolutely. With your program diagram in hand, you can begin to put ballpark figures on your big-ticket items. Having some budget figures in mind will help keep you from promising a program bigger than the budget will allow.

If you were an English major, you may have been hoping (like one of us) that you would never have to deal with math again after college. But here we all are, working in spreadsheets, entering archaic formulas to calculate annual salary increases, fringe benefits, and mileage.

Try not to think of the budget as a bunch of numbers. A detailed budget, with a clear budget narrative, tells reviewers the story of your project. It demonstrates that you are committed to thoughtful planning and have thought of every possible detail necessary for your program to be successful. Just as your logic model provides a diagram of your project, the budget and budget narrative show the reader your financial plan for the project.

As we mentioned in the previous chapter, reviewers often read your logic model and budget before they read your program narrative.

Begin Project Planning with the Budget

We know it's tempting to leave the budget for last, after the project has been planned and the narrative written. Resist. When the grants team hears that the grant allows up to $200,000 a year, that can sound like a lot of money. But if you plan out all of your activities and write a fantastic narrative only to then discover that your plans will cost $350,000 per year, you have wasted everyone's time.

Begin with the end in mind.

Bring a budget template when you begin project planning. Make sure everyone understands the budget cap or if there is a minimum budget size. Everyone also has to be crystal clear on what costs are allowable and which are unallowable.

Allowable/unallowable costs: Sometimes the RFA will explicitly state what grant funds may or may not be spent on. Anything on which you are not allowed to spend grant funds is considered "unallowable."

Budget narrative: A written description of the expenses projected in your budget.

The easiest place to start is with the most expensive items. Try to determine what the largest expenses will be. Often this is personnel. It is not unusual for personnel to take up half or even two-thirds of a grant budget, depending on the program being funded. In contrast, other programs place tight limits on allowed personnel expenditures, or they may require you to set aside a certain percentage of the budget for direct services. This can actually leave little to spend on personnel.

Once you have determined the cost of everything that is required to implement your planned program, you will have a realistic idea of how much is left to spend on equipment, supplies, or conferences. When considering the cost of "everything," don't forget to include evaluation costs, especially if your funding agency requires proof of meeting project objectives to renew your funding.

How Do We Know What Our Program Will Cost?

A grant budget is your best educated estimate of what your program will cost to implement. Organizations sometimes ask how they can develop a budget for something they've never done before. First, start with your program diagram and try to think of every possible cost to conduct your planned activities.

For example, if your plan is to inoculate 150 children against a particular disease, what sorts of supplies will you need? At least 150 of the vaccine, right? And a way to dispose of the needles, if you don't already have that. Space in

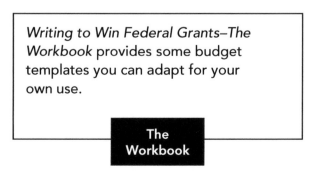

Writing to Win Federal Grants–The Workbook provides some budget templates you can adapt for your own use.

The Workbook

which to provide the inoculations. Do you have to maintain patient privacy, or will a big room work? You'll probably also need someone to give the inoculations. Does this task require an RN, or could a less costly LPN give the vaccine? How many hours will this person work? How will people know they can get the vaccine? Maybe you will need marketing materials.

For personnel, ask your HR office or payroll service to give you the salary range or hourly rate for personnel at the level you will propose. Ask for the breakdown of the fringe benefits the organization pays out too. These include payroll taxes, even if your organization has no other benefits. You are going to need this information for your budget narrative.

For supplies, such as the vaccines, research costs online or get a bid from a vendor. For something like a marketing campaign, figure out that campaign's details (are we talking television ads or a few posters?), and then price those items. You could also get advice from another organization that has implemented a similar program.

COFAR—Or The Ever-Changing Landscape of Federal Rules

The federal government has been migrating its rules for how grant funds can be spent (called "cost principles") and how grants should be managed ("administrative requirements") from documents called circulars into the Code of Federal Regulations (CFR). A "super circular" released in December 2013 announced that the requirements from the circulars have been superseded by a single new document titled "Uniform Administrative Requirements, Cost Principles, and Audit Requirements for Federal Awards." Its policies went into effect for grants awarded after December 26, 2014.

The new document is sometimes called the "final guidance." Many people simply call it COFAR. The new requirements appear in the *Federal Register* (federalregister.gov—see **Appendix K** for the full URL). COFAR simplifies and streamlines grants management rules, eliminating at least eighty pages of duplicate or conflicting guidance from the previous circulars. The updated policies are intended to ease the administrative burden on grantees while providing greater transparency and accountability.

The requirements change many important rules, including but not limited to, the threshold at which an organization must obtain an A-133 audit, how funding agencies treat indirect cost rates, and whether certain items grantees often purchase are allowable expenses (such as food). To review training webinars and for further details on the content of the Uniform Requirements, you may visit cfo.gov/cofar.

While copies of the old circulars are still available at the OMB website, they should be used only in administering grants awarded prior to December 26, 2014. When determining what costs may be allowable in future grants, or what administrative rules grantees will be required to follow, use the new super circular at the *Federal Register*.

important

Reviewers often find round numbers like $2,500 or $200 to be suspicious. They look more like guesses than "real" costs. However, do round all cents off to the nearest dollar. Do not include cents in your budget forms.

A budget checklist can help you avoid forgetting an important expense of delivering your project. For example:

◆ What does it cost to add and operate a piece of major equipment (maintenance contracts, consumable supplies)?

◆ What does it cost to take children on field trips (drivers, insurance, entrance fees)?

◆ What does it cost to add staff to your organization (salary or hourly rate, fringe benefits, furniture)?

We have included a detailed budget planning checklist in **Appendix H**. An alternate budget planning checklist appears in *Writing to Win Federal Grants–The Workbook.*

We find that no matter how carefully we think we have planned our project, when we begin writing, we always find things we forgot. It's pretty common for the program design (and, thus, the budget) to undergo one or two major changes during the planning process.

Using Federal Budget Categories

Fortunately, most federal grants use standard budget categories that you will quickly learn. And you usually enter the subtotals for each of those categories into a form in the application package. There is a "standard" form SF-424A for budgets, but your funder may ask you to use an agency-specific form or a variation on the SF-424A. Always follow specific instructions from your funding agency.

Here is our non-federalese explanation of the budget categories:

◆ *Personnel.* This includes salaries/wages of grant-funded personnel, but not independent contractors or consultants.

◆ *Fringe benefits.* This includes insurance, retirement, payroll taxes, and workers' compensation taxes. Fringe benefits are usually presented as a percentage of salaries.

Writing to Win Federal Grants–The Workbook contains two federal grant budget templates, one with space to account for matching funds.

The Workbook

Usually you want your total budget to approach the maximum amount of funding offered. If the annual budget is allowed to be $180,000, then in most cases, you want your budget request to be something like $179,979 to get as close to that $180,000 as possible. But don't do this by padding the budget or inflating costs. Reviewers will spot that a mile away!

practical tip

◆ *Travel.* Can include airfare, hotels, meals, parking, mileage, and taxis or public transportation. We usually recommend basing estimated lodging, meals, and parking on the federal per diem tables for that year. (These are available at gsa.gov/perdiem.)

◆ *Equipment.* The federal definition of equipment is any item that has an individual purchase price of more than $5,000. As strange as this may seem, since computers go into inventory at most organizations, most computers and other technology are considered supplies (not equipment) for budgeting purposes.

◆ *Supplies.* Consumable supplies such as paper or pens, but also any item with a single purchase price of less than $5,000. Therefore, you include in the supplies category any items such as computers, printers, books, or brochures.

> You may have to reformat budgets provided to you by program staff or the finance office to get expenses into the right federal budget categories.
>
>  practical tip

◆ *Contractual.* Includes costs associated with hiring independent contractors or consultants as well as contracts for services such as web design or maintenance contracts for copiers. Some RFAs direct applicants to put no items in this category, so always double-check the rules pertaining to your application.

◆ *Construction.* For those programs that allow construction or renovation expenses, those expenses go into this category.

◆ *Other.* Place into this category any item that does not clearly fall into any other category. Some RFAs direct applicants to include no items in "Other," while some RFAs list a seemingly random assortment of items that should be placed in "Other." Again, follow the specific instructions in your RFA.

Building Your Budget

Use a spreadsheet and include as much detail as you possibly can to document where the numbers came from. For example, two rows in a spreadsheet having to do with travel may look like this:

EXCERPT...

Travel	Total
DC Grantee Workshop: Airfare $500 + Meals $65 per day x 3 days ($195) + Lodging $220 x 3 days ($660) + Ground Transport/Airport Parking $15/day x 3 days ($45)	$1,400
Service Area Mileage: 1,055 miles/year x $.51/mile	$ 538
Sub-Total Travel	$1,938

This spreadsheet is what we call an "internal budget." Most of the time, it's for your use only, not for submitting with your proposal. It is what you use to calculate every single line item that you then total for the budget form. However, you may include the line items in your written budget narrative, depending on the requirements for the budget narrative and how much space you have. When you do include line items, providing the details behind a round number like $1,400 shows that your numbers are based on real prices and not just numbers you pulled from the air.

Finally, we use the internal budget to guide spending when we get the grant award. Your program will probably begin months after you submit the application. That grant budget from last year will be old news. Even if you have a memory like an elephant, what if you change jobs or get sick? What if the program director is someone new by the time you get the grant? All of that detail will be very welcome when it comes time to administer a grant that gets funded.

We can't overemphasize the importance of budgeting carefully. If you underestimate what it will cost to achieve your project objectives, you will likely be held responsible for reaching those objectives with the budget you requested. In a worst-case scenario, the grantee must find organizational funds to supplement the grant budget to complete the grant activities. Obviously, we all want to avoid that!

Budgeting for Staff Costs

The good news is that you can usually ask for staff costs in the budget. The bad news is that personnel costs can sometimes get a bit complicated to figure out. As always, you need to be up to speed on what your funding agency allows. We are talking here about general principles.

If you remember nothing else about budgeting for personnel, burn this thought into your brain: "No one can work more than 100 percent of the time." We know. Sounds weird, but you will probably have at least one argument about this with someone in your grant writing career. Put a tape flag on this page so it's handy.

Resist the urge to just type numbers into your internal budget spreadsheet. If you use formulas instead, you can immediately see the effects on the bottom line when you have to tweak the budget. And you inevitably end up doing lots of tweaking. Someone always forgets until the last minute that the software you have to buy has a required maintenance contract too, or that you have to send two people instead of only one to the grantees' conference. A quick search online will lead you to resources on using basic spreadsheet formulas, if you don't know how.

 practical tip

In grant budgets, we usually talk about staff in terms of percentage of effort. As far as the government is concerned, forty hours per week, fifty-two weeks per year (or 2,080 hours per year) is full time. That's considered 100 percent effort, or 1.0 FTE (one full-time equivalent). If a grant-funded person will work twenty hours per week on grant activities, that's a half-time person, or a 0.5 FTE.

What if your program director works more like fifty or sixty hours a week? That doesn't matter. Under a federal grant, your staff can be compensated only for the equivalent of a full-time salary. The easiest way to think about this is that staff on salary can't get a raise just because you got a federal grant, and it's very rare to be approved to pay overtime to hourly employees.

> *Percentage of effort:* A staff person who will work full time on the grant is contributing 100 percent effort. This is sometimes also written as 1.0 FTE (full-time equivalent). A person who will work ten hours per week on the grant project is dedicating 25 percent effort to the grant, or is a 0.25 FTE.

Calculating full-time equivalents works the same for staff who are paid a salary and those who are hourly employees. Your grant budget may include some of both. This is fine, as long as the pay scale matches what you do for other people in your organization.

If you put money for personnel in the personnel category, you put a corresponding number in the fringe category. You may think, "We don't have fringe benefits. We are a small organization with no insurance or retirement." Even small organizations pay payroll taxes and unemployment. These are considered fringe as far as the government is concerned.

Your human resources department or payroll service can calculate your employee's fringe benefits. They don't like to do it, but they can. Because this can get complicated for lots of reasons, they will usually provide you with an average. You would write this, for example, as "fringe benefits equal an average of 37 percent of salaries" in the budget narrative. Some organizations have one average for full-time employees and another average for part-time hourly employees.

Maybe you should take a deep breath before this next part. For lots of funders, it's expected that you be able to break this 37 percent down into all of its parts. Here is an excerpt from a real budget narrative:

EXCERPT...

The fringe benefit rate for salaried full-time personnel is 37%. This breaks down as follows: FICA 6.2%; Medicare 1.5%; State Retirement System (mandatory) 9.9%; State Unemployment .4%; worker's comp 2.7%; long-term disability .3%; short-term disability .3%; Life Insurance .4%; Health insurance 15%; and Unemployment .3% = 37%. The fringe benefit rate for instructors is 18.5%.

The higher the fringe benefits rate, the more important it is to explain what is in it. Maybe your state requires you to pay into a state retirement fund for your employees, as in the above example. Maybe your organization has a very generous health insurance policy. While 37 percent is somewhat high, it's not off the charts. The excerpt also stated that the fringe benefits is lower for instructors (who are part-time employees)—only 18.5 percent.

All of that detail, and some more information, accompanied the following table in the budget narrative. Notice that you can tell right away from the table that this project delivers some services during the academic year and others during the summers. You can tell how many people will be working on the grant project. Because the part-time instructors work only a few weeks each year, we did not discuss them in terms of percentage of effort or FTEs.

EXCERPT...

Personnel and Fringe for XYZ College Program	
Personnel	**Amount**
Project Director (100%)	$59,684
Program Coordinator (100%)	$47,119
Administrative Support Technician (100%)	$27,789
Part-Time/Temporary Personnel	
Academic Year Instructors (4 instruct. x 24 hrs/semester x $20/hr x 2 semesters)	$3,840
Summer Program Instructors (3 instructors x 20 hrs/wk x 6 wks x $20/hr)	$7,200
Subtotal Personnel	**$145,632**
Fringe Benefits for Director, Coordinator, Technician (37%)	$49,799
Fringe Benefits for Part-time Instructors (18.5%)	$2,042
Subtotal Fringe	**$51,841**

Matching Funds and In-Kind Contributions

Some federal grant programs require matching funds from the applicant. Matching funds are financial resources or the value of nonfinancial resources an applicant can contribute toward implementing grant activities.

The RFA will clearly state whether a match is required. The RFA should also state the required ratio of matching funds to federal dollars and should explain what types of contributions count toward the match.

A one-to-one match means that you must match every federal dollar with a nonfederal dollar. A two-to-one match means that for every two federal dollars requested in your budget, you must supply one nonfederal dollar (or its equivalent value if in-kind matches are allowed). Do not assume that you will be able to count state, county, or municipal funds toward a match. These may have originated at the federal level, which would mean you could not count them as part of your match.

Unless the RFA states otherwise, matching funds do not have to be in cash. Noncash matches are called "in-kind contributions." You have many options for coming up with in-kind matches. In addition to goods or cash that may be contributed to your project by third parties, you may also count the value of volunteer time. (See the sidebar on the next page for tips on how to do this.)

> *Matching funds:* Cash or in-kind value of resources provided by the applicant to match the federal grant amount being requested. If the match ratio is one-to-one and you receive a $50,000 grant, the applicant organization must contribute or obtain cash or $50,000 worth of goods and services and apply those to the grant budget as well.
>
> **definition**

If you list the value of your own personnel as in-kind, that usually means that they will be spending time relating to the grant project in some way but you are not "charging" their time to the grant's budget. For example, your executive director may spend five hours a week dealing with paperwork or supervising the project director, but you have not included this person's time in the grant budget. You can then consider 12.5 percent of the executive director's time (five hours equals 12.5 percent of forty hours) and fringe benefits as part of your in-kind match.

Example items commonly used to meet in-kind matches include the following:

◆ Value of personnel time spent on the project (must be personnel with direct activities related to the grant whose wages are not paid by the grant, such as people who spend 5 percent of their time supervising a project director)

◆ Value of volunteer hours contributed to the project

◆ Value of space contributed to the project, such as office space (ask your accountant or business office for a per-square-foot value of space the project will use at your organization)

◆ Value of furnishings project personnel will use for project activities, such as desks, chairs, computers, telephones, etc.

> You can put a dollar amount on the value of time volunteers contribute to your project activities. For volunteers doing something outside their normal jobs (such as a CPA building a house), you can value their time based on the current rate as calculated by the Independent Sector (independentsector.org).
>
> For volunteers contributing time in their professional capacity, such as US federal judges mentoring Chinese judges (yes, that was one of our projects), you may base the value of their time on the Department of Labor pay scale for that position.
>
>  practical tip

◆ Value of utilities or access to the Internet that the grant-funded project will receive through your organization

◆ Value of the use of an organization-owned vehicle while performing grant-related duties, if the vehicle use is not included in the grant budget as a direct cost

◆ Value of services provided by another organization

The chart below is an excerpt from an internal budget spreadsheet. This excerpt shows in-kind values applied to a required applicant match. Notice how well documented most of the cost estimates are. Eventually, these numbers and the descriptions for how each amount was reached were also included in the budget narrative.

EXCERPT...

	Federal	Non-Federal Match	Total Project Costs
Personnel			
Project Director (50% FTE) (50% of annual salary of $140,000)	$70,000		$70,000
Program Coordinator (100% FTE)	$35,000		$35,000
Administrative Assistant (10% FTE—in-kind)		$2,850	$2,850
Sub-Total Personnel	$105,000	$2,850	$107,850
C. Supplies			
Five Computers (5 @ $850/ea.)	$4,250		$4,250
Office supplies (avg. $75/month x 12 months)		$900	$900
Sub-Total Supplies	$4,250	$900	$5,150

For something to count as an in-kind match, you need to be able to calculate its value and track its "expenditure" during the grant project period. Do not overestimate the value of in-kind contributions. Any funds or resources promised to the federal agency as part of a required match legally become federal resources. In the case of a cash match, you must be able to document that funds were transferred to the grant account.

For in-kind matches, keep clear documentation that the promised space was really used by the grant program, an inventory of the promised furnishings, or a time sheet of in-kind time spent on grant activities by nongrant personnel.

It is important to understand the difference between a required match and what is commonly called "evidence of applicant's commitment," or "leverage." Required matching funds are included on the SF-424A form and must be accounted for just as you account for grant funds.

If you are asked only to provide evidence of the applicant's commitment to a project, you can discuss the value of such contributions in the grant narrative, but do not include the dollar values on the SF-424A form in the official budget.

Anything reported in the "Applicant" column on the SF-424A is considered by federal agencies to be "their" money and is auditable. So never include actual dollar amounts in the that column unless a match is required.

> Several sample time and effort worksheets as well as a donated goods tracking sheet are included in *Writing to Win Federal Grants–The Workbook*. The workbook also provides a sample budget form SF-424A with instructions for filling it out properly.
>
> **The Workbook**

Budget Narratives

Since you enter totals only for each federal budget category onto the SF-424A form, the budget narrative is where you provide the line-item budget detail for each category. You then "narrate" your budget. Follow the same order as the budget itself. The budget narrative walks reviewers line by line through your planned budget and explains several important things:

◆ What expenditures will be for (what you are buying)

◆ How you arrived at your cost estimates (written bid, per diem tables, past experience, etc.)

◆ The math behind totals (how many items you are buying, at what cost each)

◆ How budget items are directly linked to project activities and outcomes

◆ Why costs are reasonable

Make sure there are no surprises in your budget! When serving as a grant reviewer, Cheryl once encountered a grant budget that set aside several thousand dollars for website development. It was probably a reasonable cost, given the project design.

Unfortunately, the project narrative never mentioned the need for a website. It never said there was a marketing strategy that included a website or anything else that would help reviewers understand how a website fit into the project design.

As a result, the reviewers awarded a lower score to that applicant's budget. Losing even one point can cause your application to not get funded.

stories from the real world

Explain anything that has the potential to confuse reviewers. We particularly make it a point to explain costs that we think a reviewer might think are high. Airfare in travel budgets is often high if the staff must fly from rural areas without discount carriers. Once we had a client whose location was so rural that the staff had to drive hundreds of miles to the nearest airport. This required an overnight stay because of the limited flight schedules out of that small airport. We don't know where our reviewers are from, but if we happen to get a panel of urban dwellers, used to choosing from among three airports all within one hour of their apartments, an overnight hotel stay just to catch a flight will need explaining in the budget narrative.

You can also use the budget narrative to explain the absence of an expense reviewers might be expecting to see in the budget. Such absences usually occur because the organization has another strategy to meet this expense. But don't expect your reviewers to know that. For example, we once added a note to a budget narrative that the applicant was going to provide transportation to program participants using its own vehicles at its own expense. Because we had discussed transportation obstacles in the need section, reasonable reviewers would have expected to see transportation costs in the budget. Reviewers could not possibly know that we were going to take care of transportation ourselves if we did not tell them.

Another important function of your budget narrative is to provide details for how you came up with figures (see the sample budget excerpts provided earlier in this chapter). Unless our space is extremely limited, we provide as much detail as possible, down to the number of units to be purchased and the unit price.

Always double-check that the project narrative refers to major budget items or sets up a reasonable explanation for a particular item that appears in the budget. For example, if your budget will include funds for a marketing campaign, make sure that your project narrative describes your planned marketing activities. If an item other than general office supplies appears in your budget, always

Writing to Win Federal Grants–The Workbook includes a complete budget narrative from a sample proposal.

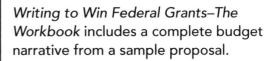

The Workbook

go back and review your project narrative to be sure you've told reviewers how that item contributes to your project activities.

The excerpt below includes the travel budget that was first presented earlier in this chapter. This time the budget figures are accompanied by the budget narrative that was written to explain the line-item expenditures. Our federal budget narratives include both the narrative description and the line-item detail that we take right out of our internal budget spreadsheet. The capital letter "C" and the subheading "Travel" both align with the federal budget categories from an SF-424A form.

EXCERPT...

C. Travel

Travel funds are set aside for the Project Director to attend the required Grantees' Workshop in Washington, D.C. Lodging and meals are based on federal per diem allowances; airfare is based on average coach travel from the XYZ Regional Airport. Additional funds are budgeted for staff travel within the six-county service area. The mileage rate is based on the IRS-approved rate for 2012.

Travel	Federal	Total
DC Grantee Workshop: Airfare $500 + Meals $65 per day x 3 days ($195) + Lodging $220 x 3 days ($660) + Ground Transport/Airport Parking $15/day x 3 days ($45)	$1,400	$1,400
Service Area Mileage: 1,055 miles/year x $.51/mile	$538	$538
Sub-Total Travel	$1,938	$1,938

If your organization does not have its own per diem rates, then you can base your expected lodging and meals expenses on the approved federal per diem table for that year. You can look these up at the General Services Administration at gsa.gov/perdiem. Similarly, if your organization does not set its own mileage reimbursement rate, you can base your budget on the current year's rate published by the IRS. Go to irs.gov and search for mileage rates on the site or conduct a web search for "IRS mileage rates 20xx."

In sum, carefully thought-out budgets and well-written budget narratives accomplish the following:

◆ Present total costs of the project

◆ Demonstrate the project is well planned

◆ Make clear what portion the funder is being asked to support

◆ Indicate the organization's support of the project

Direct costs: Expenses that can be clearly attributed to a specific grant-funded project, such as the salary for the project's director or the costs of medical supplies used to perform health screenings.

Indirect costs (sometimes called facilities and administrative costs or overhead costs): Costs of delivering a grant that are less directly attributable to any single project and are more often considered "the cost of doing business," such as the cost of the accounting department to process grant expenses.

◆ Direct the project after it's funded

◆ Tie the project expenditures to the goals and objectives

Direct and Indirect Costs

Up until this point, all of the expenditures we have been describing are considered "direct costs." Direct costs are items that can be easily accounted for as grant expenses—the supplies that must be purchased to deliver project activities or the travel to the required grant recipients' workshop. In general, direct costs are things that directly touch or benefit a participant.

You can also sometimes request indirect costs in your budget. Indirect costs are other expenses an organization incurs to manage and deliver a grant project. They are sometimes called facilities and administrative costs or overhead costs. That is because indirect costs are harder to apply precisely to any single grant project.

Typical indirect costs may include the time of the human resources office to hire and process grant-funded staff members or for the accounts payable department to track and pay all of a grant's invoices. The expense of heating and cooling the space to be allocated to the project might be considered an indirect cost.

The Code of Federal Regulations (CFR) explained earlier in this chapter contains the rules regarding what types of expenses are considered direct costs and what types are indirect costs. However, be aware that total direct costs plus indirect costs may not exceed the grant award ceiling.

Indirect Cost Rate Details

An applicant organization has to submit extensive paperwork to the proper federal agency to request an indirect cost rate determination. Once the rate has been set,

If you are applying for only one federal grant, or your first federal grant, it is not likely to be worth the effort to go through the process of trying to negotiate an approved federal indirect cost rate. In fact, you are in a catch-22. Most of the time, you are not allowed to request an indirect cost rate until you have already won at least one federal grant. The new COFAR attempts to resolve this by allowing applicants to request a minimum indirect cost rate of 10 percent if they do not already have a negotiated rate. However, certain exceptions to the 10 percent rule are allowed, so obtain program officer verification if the RFA is unclear on how to request indirect costs.

this is your indirect cost rate for all federal agencies. The regulations issued in December 2013 are supposed to force federal agencies to honor your indirect cost rate, except in certain circumstances. It also establishes that organizations without a negotiated rate may request 10 percent in indirect costs.

Regardless of what rate is set for your organization, some grant programs currently exclude indirect costs, meaning that you can include only direct costs in your budget. Other agencies currently cap indirect costs at a rate of 8 or 10 percent of your total direct costs. If this happens, you can claim the difference between your approved rate and the capped rate as part of your matching funds, if they are required.

> If your organization does not have an indirect-cost rate or if the agency to whom you are applying has capped indirect costs at less than your negotiated rate, then maximize direct costs as much as possible. If you can dig deeply and track or determine how much photocopying the grant will use or how much extra custodial expenses your organization will incur because of grant activities, put those costs into the grant budget.

If your organization has only one federal grant under management at any one time, such expenses would not seem particularly burdensome. However, once an organization is large enough to be managing several government grants and contracts simultaneously, then the burdens on the accounting staff or other administrative systems begin to be felt.

Usually there is no need for an organization to attempt to negotiate an indirect-cost rate if its federal grant income is less than $1 million per year. Once an organization grows to managing significant federal grant revenue annually, it is time to consider submitting an indirect-cost-rate proposal.

Such a proposal is submitted by your organization's financial personnel. Most organizations work with outside financial consultants experienced with indirect cost rate proposals to help them through this complicated process.

This brief explanation only scratches the surface of how indirect costs work. A bit more thorough introduction, written from the perspective of what the grant professional needs to understand about indirect costs, is found at Grants Northwest, at grantsnorthwest.com/indirect-costs-in-federal-grants.

To Recap

◆ Good grant budgets help tell the story of your project.

◆ Your budget and budget narrative help assure reviewers that your project is planned carefully.

◆ Combined direct and indirect costs must remain within the maximum allowable grant amount.

◆ The budget must be clearly aligned with project activities and should include no surprises for reviewers.

◆ The budget narrative explains planned expenditures for reviewers and helps reviewers determine if the budget is realistic.

Chapter Eight

Tackling the Blank Page: How to Start Writing

IN THIS CHAPTER

- ┄➔ Using the RFA to guide your writing
- ┄➔ Tips about writing style
- ┄➔ Making it easy for reviewers to award you points
- ┄➔ Little RFA quirks to watch out for

Finally. Now we let you start writing. Earlier we referred to skimming an RFA for the information to help you decide whether to apply as speed dating. Now that you are going to start writing, this relationship is getting serious. You have to meet the crazy uncle and learn all of the family secrets. No more skirting around the edges.

Now your entire life is about points. Your top priority is to make reviewers' jobs easy. Their job is to award (or not award) points to your proposal. The guidelines provide you with the best road map to what the reviewers will be looking for in each section of your proposal.

Start Writing from the Evaluation Criteria

While we insist you read the entire RFA, we are going to jump right to the section you will spend the most time with, the evaluation criteria. Not to be confused with the evaluation plan, the evaluation criteria tell you how applications will be scored. If you are lucky, the criteria will even spell out how many points are awarded to each subcriterion.

To make it easy for reviewers to find every item they are looking for, create section headings directly from the evaluation criteria (unless the RFA says something different). Make the

What do you do when the RFA does not offer clear evaluation criteria? Dig through the RFA looking for any instructions regarding what should be included in your narrative or to see if the agency provides a separate proposal writing guide (like the National Science Foundation). Sometimes the RFA will have only a chart that lists major sections. Sometimes a copy of the federal regulations is included in the RFA with content like "How does the secretary determine need?" Other times, you may just have to organize your content in the way that makes the most sense to you. Then be sure to use titles and subheadings liberally.

practical tip

headings bold or underline them. Make it impossible for reviewers to miss the fact that you answered every question.

This is important because most funding agencies take the evaluation criteria and turn them into a scoring rubric for reviewers.

You should do your best to ensure reviewers never have to search for information. Searching for information annoys readers, and annoyed readers award fewer points. Maybe we should all have posters on our walls that read, "Don't annoy the reviewers." Its pair would say, "Help the reviewers give you points!"

The excerpt below includes part of the evaluation criteria from an RFA. Get familiar with the main points of this excerpt. We are going to refer back to this example more than once.

EXCERPT...

OBJECTIVES AND NEED FOR ASSISTANCE - 10 pts
An application will be evaluated on the extent to which it demonstrates that the organization is established and has well-developed connections to and working relationships with the nonprofit community in the well-defined geographic area they propose to serve.

(a)Service Area (2 Points). An application will be evaluated on the extent to which the applicant identifies a specific, well-defined service area for project implementation. An application will be evaluated on the extent to which the applicant demonstrates a prior history of involvement in and connectedness to the proposed service area.

Writing Outline

When you sit down to write your proposal, your first task should be to turn these evaluation criteria into a writing outline:

EXCERPT...

I. Objectives and Need for Assistance
  A. Service Area (2 pts.)
    i. Specific, well-defined service area
    ii. Prior history of involvement in and connectedness to service area

Follow this process throughout the entire evaluation criteria. Your outline may be two or three pages long. But someone has provided it for you! You do not have to come up with this stuff on your own.

See *Writing to Win Federal Grants–The Workbook* for a sample of a reviewer's scoring matrix drawn from an RFA.

The Workbook

Criteria as Topic Sentences

When you begin writing content to complete the outline, use the wording from the RFA as subheadings and as topic sentences for major paragraphs. Here is an example of the first few sentences written in response to the excerpted RFA above. We have added the underlining in this sample to highlight how this text responds directly to the RFA text:

EXCERPT...

Service Area and Prior History of Involvement

The <u>specific service area</u> to be served by this project consists of Benton, Carroll, Madison and Washington counties Arkansas. [Include a map if you can.]

The Do Good Community Foundation has <u>a prior history of involvement in and connectedness to the service area</u> because it has been located in Benton County since 1992. Through our Nonprofit Capacity Building program, we have served 120 nonprofit organizations in the service area by…(and you would name the services you have provided here and go into more detail about how you are connected to the community).

Subpoint ii under "A. Service Area" says applicants must "demonstrate a prior history of involvement in and connectedness to service area." How do you demonstrate this? Take a look back at the excerpt. Even though the sentences preceding the subhead "A. Service Area" have no points attached to them, they can give you hints about what should be included in a complete response.

When you first start filling in your outline with content, you can use bullet points or brainstormed thoughts. Your main task is to get all the information in the right place, under the correct heading. You can go back and polish the prose later.

practical tip

Those sentences say that reviewers are going to be looking for evidence that applicants are "established" (this means you should talk about your long track record of success in the community). They are also looking for proof that the organization has "well-developed connections to and working relationships with the nonprofit community." So it would be essential to describe all of the ways you have partnered with other agencies in your proposed service area or other history of services provided in that area.

Repetitive Content and Cross-References

You may find that some content is requested more than once. For example, in a recent application, we were asked to address the sustainability of project activities under two different criteria: "impact" and "applicant resources and capabilities."

See *Writing to Win Federal Grants–The Workbook* for the complete evaluation criteria from this RFA and the outline we created in response.

The Workbook

The best strategy in such situations is to answer the question both times if space allows. Reread the RFA text very carefully to ensure that there are not different emphases to sections that may appear at first glance to be identical. For example, in the case of sustainability, one section may be asking you to address the sustainability of the grant-funded project, while another section may be asking you to address the organization's overall long-term sustainability.

If there is no significant difference in the duplicate evaluation criteria, express your point a little differently in each section. You may point reviewers back to the previous section with a cross-reference, such as: "Please see page 24 for the plan for sustaining network activities after federal support has ended." But then add a summary of the previous section's major points if possible.

Some funders tell their reviewers that each section of a proposal has to stand on its own. If the content is not found in that section (even if there is a cross-reference), the reviewer is told to award no points. Other funders are not as strict. Some tell reviewers they have to give you the points if the information is found anywhere in the narrative. We prefer not to risk it.

Remember, your number-one job is to make the reviewers' jobs easy. If they are following their scoring rubric in order, they want to find your content in order. You will likely never know if the agency you are applying to is one of those that is a real stickler for exactly where the information must be found.

Let any internal reviewers at your organization know to expect repetition in your narrative and what may even seem like illogical organization. If you can, provide the evaluation criteria with your draft so they understand why your narrative is organized the way it is. This will save you and them a lot of time spent on needless editing to "improve" the narrative.

practical tip

Telling the Reviewer to Award You Points

The outline is the first step in the writing process. Then you start filling it in with content. When you write, repeat the criteria back to your readers. As was described above, you accomplish this by using the criteria as your subheadings. Your topic sentences also repeat the text from the RFA in a clear statement of how you meet these criteria.

In the example below of text composed in response to the RFA excerpt, the underlined text represents text that was lifted from the RFA language for repeating back to the reviewer. More important than simply repeating the words from the criteria, your sentence comes right out and says that the applicant "has a prior history of involvement."

In other words, make it as easy as possible for that reviewer to tick the box on the scoring rubric that says "involvement in and connectedness to service area."

EXCERPT...

Service Area

The <u>specific service area</u> to be served by this project consists of Benton, Carroll, Madison and Washington counties Arkansas. [Include a map if you can.]

The Do Good Community Foundation has <u>a prior history of involvement in and connectedness to the service area</u> because it has been located in Benton County since 1992. Through our Nonprofit Capacity Building program, we have served 120 nonprofit organizations in the service area by . . .

This is what we mean by "telling" the reviewer to award you points. Include several assertions that you meet the specific criteria. Then follow up with specific examples. The paragraph from which this sample was taken continued on, offering examples of involvement and connectedness. And, yes, we kept using those two terms repeatedly to tell the reviewer that we were meeting that criterion.

After you claim to meet a criterion, explain why. Give specific examples, with numbers if possible. Tell a story. Include a quotation in a box from someone you have served.

Make your writing style clear, direct, and as easy to understand as possible. Federal reviewers are wading through huge stacks of complex proposals. They are tired. It is easy for them to start skimming or to overlook essential content if you do not make it stand out. Use lots of subheadings, and sometimes emphasize a point with boldface or underlining.

It is always best to assume that reviewers have no knowledge of your field of expertise. They may even be unfamiliar with the funding opportunity. Don't be condescending in your writing, but also explain everything thoroughly. And don't use a single acronym without explaining what it is first! We sometimes go so far as to spell out important acronyms at least once in each section to eliminate any possible confusion.

!
important

First Person versus Third Person

We often get asked if writing in first person is acceptable. It is. Unless, of course, your grant guidelines instruct you otherwise. We do know of a few instances in which this the case. However, the rest of the time, we usually write in first person and consistently win big federal grants every year. We have learned two important things: (1) first person is usually easier for readers to understand, and (2) it takes fewer words. Space is always at a premium.

One reason first person takes less space on the page (and less energy from the reader) is that you don't have to keep saying "the organization will" or "the Starlight School will" or "the applicant will." All you have to say is "we will." First person allows you to talk with, rather than at, the reviewer. Sometimes that level of comfort scores points.

We often use small quote boxes from clients, patients, or students that contribute to the picture of need or of the project's potential impact. They just don't usually have as primary a role as they might have in a foundation proposal.

The excerpt below compares text written to describe a grant applicant. The first example is written in third person and contains forty-one words. The second example is written in first person. It requires only thirty-four words to convey the same information as the first example. More importantly, this edit saved an entire line of text.

EXCERPT...

Third person:
The Northwest Arkansas Women's Shelter serves more than 4,000 people each year through the shelter's in-shelter and outreach services. The Shelter will measure the outcomes of people staying in the shelter each year to assess the effectiveness of the organization's programs. (41 words)

Rewritten in first person:
We serve more than 4,000 people each year through our in-shelter and outreach services. We will measure the outcomes of people staying in the shelter each year to assess the effectiveness of our programs. (34 words)

Of course, the accepted style for most research proposals remains third person. These are a specific type of proposal. It's unlikely you will ever be uncertain about whether you are writing or editing a research proposal as opposed to a program or other sort of proposal.

What Would You Do for a Line of Text?

If you don't understand the question posed in the title of this section, you have never tried to cram one hundred pages of content into forty-five pages. Apparently, some people have tried some desperate measures over the years to squeeze every single word of their brilliant prose into the margins. We suspect that a lot of the crazy rules we encounter in federal guidelines were developed in response to some of these desperate measures.

Here are a few extremely directive rules, right out of real RFAs. Go ahead, quiz yourself and see how many you would have been tempted to try.

◆ All space in a document must be double-spaced, even charts, tables, and footnotes. (Can we just say that double-spaced tables and footnotes are almost impossible to read? And have you ever tried to force your word processor to produce double-spaced footnotes? Thankfully, we think the reviewers rose up en masse that year in protest, because the next year, we could single space our tables again.)

◆ "Use one of the following fonts: Times New Roman, Courier, Courier New, or Arial. Applications submitted in any other font (including Times Roman and Arial Narrow) will not be accepted." We doubt you will ever be tempted to try to save space by using Courier, but go ahead try it now. We'll wait. Not such a great strategy, is it? Most word processors do have a feature to "compress" your letters horizontally, so you can sneak more words onto each line and technically still be using a twelve-point font, which must have been the inspiration for the next bullet.

◆ "Use a font that is either 12 point or larger, and no smaller than 10 pitch (characters per inch)." If you think federal agency staff members getting out their rulers to measure how many lines of text are on a page or to make sure your table doesn't bleed a teensy bit into the left or right margins sounds too Kafkaesque to be true, we kind of hate to burst your bubble. It happens.

> One of the most difficult federal proposals we ever wrote was only two pages long. With such limited space, we had to seriously pare down every single word. We won—two years in a row. More is not always better.
>
> **stories from the real world**

◆ Sometimes the funder feels the need to define "double space" by adding this detail: "Double space (no more than three lines per vertical inch) all text in the application narrative." Remember what we said about rulers?

I suppose if we were technically savvy enough to attempt one of those maneuvers, we would have used them ourselves. Here are some strategies we do use that have not yet been outlawed—at least not by every funding agency:

◆ Edit, edit, and edit some more. Usually, shorter words are more precise anyway— such as "teach" or "lead" instead of "facilitate." Some people call this not using a "dollar" word when a "nickel" word works just as well. Some writers dislike the style guide written by Strunk and White, but one of us (we're not saying which one) still returns to it now and again for a refresher on cutting out unnecessary adjectives and other tips for being concise.

◆ Make sacrifices. We almost drove our editors crazy, but in some of the excerpts included in this book, we wanted you to see some of the sacrifices we have made to the grammar and punctuation gods to get text to fit inside a table, so you can see how far you can push the boundaries and still get funded. Some of our tricks include

The number of points allocated to different sections of the proposal can serve as a good guide to how many pages to dedicate to each section. Sections worth ten points probably should be more fully developed (meaning longer) than sections worth only two points.

practical tip

leaving periods off of abbreviations and forcing words to be hyphenated in strange spots. We usually break the rules about spelling out numbers because we want them to stand out (takes up less space too).

◆ Fiddle with the internal margins of table cells. You can stretch your text right up to the inside edge of a table cell.

◆ Put complex concepts into tables. As we explain in **Chapter Eleven**, trying to describe a long process of several steps in narrative form eats up a lot of valuable real estate.

◆ When you have a paragraph that has only one word in the final line, you can usually reword something earlier in the paragraph to move that last word up one line. Some writers follow a rule of thumb that a line needs five or more words to be worth the space it's taking up.

When you have written the narrative and included thorough responses to all of the queries posed to you by the guidelines, it can be hard to imagine how to make that shorter. That is why we have all spent hours trying to shave off one word here or abbreviate a citation to make it shorter there. We will stay up until 3:00 a.m. to find something to cut in a paragraph to save a line of text.

Keep the Applicant's Name Front and Center

Despite the need to be brief, repeat your organization's name frequently. Do not fall into the bad habit of writing out your organization's name once on the first page and then referring to it only by its acronym on the remaining seventy-nine pages. We recommend repeating your organization's name, or a shortened version of your name, as often as every other page.

Reviewers must read and score a large stack of proposals. They have to keep multiple applicants straight in their heads. The proposals begin to look the same, and the applicants do too. If your organization's official name is Susan G. Komen for the Cure Ozark Affiliate, you will lose valuable "real estate" if you must write that name out over and over again.

So call yourself "Susan G. Komen" or "the Komen Ozark Affiliate" to differentiate your organization from all of those other affiliates. Either is much more memorable than referring to yourself as "SGKOA" or something similarly awkward throughout a lengthy proposal.

What about Graphics and Photos?

Graphics and photos, used sparingly, can be worth the valuable real estate they take up, as long as they are allowed by the guidelines. Remember though that reviewers may see any illustrations or photos only in black and white. Make sure black and white versions of your images are clear. They often aren't.

As you will see in the next chapter, we sometimes include a map that illustrates the service area. We have used photos too, if they seemed important to illustrate either the great need for the project or to help explain what it is we plan to do with the money. "Before" shots can work well to demonstrate need in renovation projects. We've also seen photos used in proposals to show how an innovative classroom design works or to show what an expensive item of equipment looks like.

Some RFA "Gotchas" to Watch Out For

While it is essential to base your writing outline on the evaluation criteria, do not make the mistake of zeroing in on that portion of the RFA and writing only in response to what you find there.

Some RFAs sneak in two sets of criteria. There might be a whole section elsewhere in the RFA that says "when demonstrating need, applications should discuss…." Then they do this for each major section, such as organizational capacity, quality of personnel, and the budget.

Usually there will be no points assigned to these instructions. Do not ignore them, though. We strongly recommend that you follow the order of the evaluation criteria, but allow yourself to depart from that outline if you need to squeeze in something from the other instructions.

Often there is no real conflict. The "extra" guidelines just mean that you need to include "extra" content. Your challenge will be the find the place that makes the most sense to work this into your writing outline.

Similar to these alternate instructions, any part of an RFA may include some essential requirement. Maybe the RFA mentions somewhere that you have to certify that all curriculum used by your project is in the public domain. Or perhaps you are required to include a statement that says you promise to participate in the agency's prescribed evaluation process.

Read the RFA with a fine-toothed comb, expecting to find surprising nuggets. Sometimes such surprises may require you to rethink your strategy. Other times, you may find details that require a response that doesn't fit neatly into your outline, and the RFA does not tell you where to place it. Then you have to think strategically about where to place your response in the narrative so that reviewers can find it without it intruding unnecessarily in the

Don't start writing in response to what looks like instructions for what content should be in your proposal if these instructions aren't clearly labeled as the evaluation criteria. Some RFAs contain more than one set of instructions. When that happens, the safest strategy is to find the most logical way possible to include responses to both sets of instructions in your narrative.

Reading the Fine Print of RFAs

Karen was once working with an applicant who had started a grant proposal to expand an existing program providing early learning services for at-risk infants and toddlers. The proposal narrative was almost complete, except for the evaluation plan. Then a member of the team noticed for the first time one line in the RFA. It was only one line, but it was a deal killer.

Organizations whose proposals were for program expansions were not allowed to spend budget funds on evaluation. The project director was shocked to learn that the required evaluation would have to be paid for from the organization's own funds since it was not proposing a new program. The organization had insufficient funds in its budget to cover the evaluation costs, so it had to pull the plug on that application. Had the program director been aware of that important requirement earlier, the organization still would not have been able to submit an application, but weeks of work would have been saved.

flow of your text. We have been known to put extra assurances at the very end of the narrative when they did not seem to fit anywhere else. And we put a very big subheading on there to make sure reviewers saw it.

To Recap

◆ Use the evaluation criteria to create your proposal outline.

◆ Use outline contents as topic sentences.

◆ Make it easy for reviewers to award you all points.

◆ Scour the RFA for hidden requirements or alternate instructions.

Chapter Nine

Proposal Sections: Need

IN THIS CHAPTER

···→ Painting a picture of need

···→ Making it easier to understand complex data

···→ Where to find data for your need section

Once, when we were working with an organization on its need section, the organization's staff members got a little frustrated. They told us they would not be spending their time to write this proposal if they didn't need the grant. The reviewers should know that.

Well, yes. But, then, those 565 other applicants you are competing against need the grant too. Why do you need it worse than they do? What do you say to reviewers to help them evaluate the need in your community versus that of someone else's town?

It may be tempting to think the need for your organization's services is obvious. You see firsthand every day the problems or gaps in your community. You can envision how your arts or educational programming or the flood-plain mitigation project can improve the quality of life in your service area.

But the reviewers do not know your community. In fact, they were probably purposefully selected from an entirely different region of the country. A great need statement describes clearly the community to be served and paints a picture of need so that reviewers who don't know you or the people you serve can understand why your project is needed in the community.

Not every RFA will use the words "need statement." Sometimes you may be asked to describe the problems facing your community. Or you may be asked to discuss the weaknesses in an existing system or organization. Regardless of what terms are used, your job is to prove that your community needs this grant to make life there better. But first, you usually have to describe your project's service area or the population to be served.

Defining the Service Area and Target Population

While these issues are not themselves a "need," we usually describe the need in the context of the geographic area to be served by the grant or the people who will be served by or benefit from the grant. If you are proposing to add environmental education features to a public green space, then your target population may be all of the residents of your city or county—in addition to the students who will study the public area's environmental characteristics. If you are a federally qualified health center (FQHC), your target population is low-income patients. Your service area will be the counties or zip codes recognized by the Department of Health and Human Services as your territory.

Sometimes defining a service area is relatively easy. Maybe yours is limited by certain counties, or by the city limits. But most social service and arts organizations don't have a geographically limited service areas. So their service areas may be defined as wherever those they serve come from. Arts organizations are fortunate enough to have the zip codes of their ticket-purchasing patrons, and hospitals have the zip codes of their patients. Other organizations must use other methods, such as constituent surveys, to determine the reach of their services.

> We have been using the term "community" as a loose term to mean your service area. You may serve a single city or county, you may have a five-county service area, or you may belong to a multistate, or even international, consortium.
>
>

> *Service area*: The geographic area, such as county, state, city, or group of census tracts, that is the focus of your proposed program's services. This is not necessarily the same as where your organization is located. Other terms for this include target area or community to be served.
>
> *Target population*: Those to be served by the grant, sometimes limited by a factor such as age or income level, or defined by a segment of the population such as individuals diagnosed with a mental illness. The target population may include all people within the service area or some portion of the population.
>
>

If you must define a service area for the purposes of your application, unless the RFA gives you other instructions, you usually have great freedom to determine how you do this. You can use zip codes, census tracts, school districts, or whatever other designation makes sense for you. As long as you clearly state how you defined your service area, this is an acceptable approach to take.

The example below is an excerpt from one proposal that used zip codes and census tracts to define the area served. In this particular proposal, the census tracts were important because they were also the source of the demographic information used later in the proposal. All Census data is available free online. Most writers of government proposals become experts at using the Census Bureau's online data system, or they become good friends with such an expert, such as a librarian.

EXCERPT...

The community of Affton is located in unincorporated South St. Louis County. The Affton community is loosely defined by a variety of boundaries including the 63123 zip code, the Affton School District, and specific streets (Watson Road to the North, to Laclede Station Road to the West, from Gravois Road to approximately I-55 on the South, and then nearly to the St. Louis boundary to the East). For the purposes of this narrative, the census tracts of 2197, 2198, 2199, 2200, 2206.01, 2207.01, and 2208.01 were used to obtain 2005 Census data.

As you can tell, if you have no familiarity with the community being described by that excerpt above, giving you the names of those roads and saying that they are the boundaries of the applicant's service area doesn't help very much. That's why we use maps whenever they are allowed and we have space. Maps can be a good visual tool that can instantly show a reader what is hard to communicate with words only.

The excerpt below illustrates how a very small locator map was placed alongside text that described the proposed reach of a multipartner consortium. Each of the partners had satellite locations and other partnerships that would enable their programs to reach farther west than their home locations as they are indicated on the map.

EXCERPT...

The application from which this sample was drawn had extremely short page limits, so the service area description is probably one of the briefest we've ever written.

The Southern Arizona Consortium's service area has more than 1.5 million residents in its 22,000 square miles, more than Massachusetts and Vermont combined. The map illustrates this area and locates the main campus of each institution. Together we can develop a regional solution to enabling displaced workers to earn certificates or degrees more quickly and at higher rates of success.

Narrowing Down Your Need Story

Once the reviewers understand whom you plan to serve and where those people live and work, it's time to explain the need you are trying to address. Standout proposals paint such a clear picture of need that by the time reviewers get to your program description, they should be thinking, "Wow, what that town really needs is..." And there you are, with the perfect solution.

Funders Don't Care What You Need

Be sure your need section describes a need in the community, not your organization's need. For example, you may be proposing a cancer-screening project. The program people might have said something to you like, "We need to hire two radiology techs." You, the brilliant grant professional, translate that into, "Our community really needs more cancer screenings." The data you provide and the stories you tell in the need section will paint the need for cancer screenings. The staff are merely the means to meet the need. They aren't the need.

important

This may feel a bit overwhelming. All communities face an array of serious needs. The good news is you have to focus on only two things: (1) any items the RFA specifically requires you to discuss, and (2) any additional items directly linked to your proposed activities.

Don't spend a lot of time in your need section describing a need that your project cannot address. For example, if your program will address the growing obesity epidemic in your community, then don't build your need story around high rates of smoking or drunk driving.

In each of the two excerpts from RFAs that are provided below, information about what we would call the need is worth fifteen points. In the first example, the RFA comes right out and calls this need.

EXCERPT...

Criterion 1: NEED (15 points)
  a.) The applicant clearly identifies and establishes the unmet health care needs of the target population as evidenced by:
    i. data regarding the incidence in the target population through demographic information, health disparities etc., relevant to the project.
    ii. the extent to which the applicant illustrates the target population to be served. The applicant provides supporting local, state, and national data for the community and the target population and compares local data versus state and national data.

Did you notice that there were some pretty specific recommendations about the type of data you would include in your project narrative? Take a look at the final sentence, which instructs applicants to make sure they compare their local data against state and national data. We recommend you do this as much as possible, even if the RFA does not come right out and require it.

In the second RFA excerpt below, we had to dig a little. The Environmental Protection Agency actually never got around to asking for a traditional need section in this RFA. But buried in a section called "scope of work" were prompts that told us how the funding agency expects its applicants to describe their community and its environmental problems that need to be addressed.

EXCERPT...	
Criteria	Points
3. Disproportionately Impacted Communities Under this criterion, the Agency will evaluate the extent to which the proposed project is likely to benefit segments of the population that are or have been traditionally disproportionately and/or adversely impacted by environmental hazards or risks, such as minorities, children or low-income individuals as described in Section 1.B.	10
4. Community Effect: Under this criterion, the Agency will evaluate the extent to which the proposed project activities address environmental and/or public health concerns affecting the community or region where the project is to be performed.	5

The table makes it clear that our community description must include the following information:

◆ Who is in the population we propose to serve (demographic information)

◆ Proof that the population in our target area consists of "minorities, children, or low-income individuals" or another group that we can demonstrate has been disproportionately "impacted by environmental hazards"

◆ What the environmental or public health concerns are that affect the community/ region we propose to serve

Notice these two RFAs approach the issue of need, or community problem, from different perspectives. But they are also asking for some similar types of information. Our tip for making sure you earn every single point is to dissect RFAs the way we did with our bullet list. List out every item separated from the rest by a comma or other punctuation, and work your way down the list.

Telling Your Need Story

You have your marching orders. The RFA has laid out all of the information you are expected to include in your need section. One of the biggest challenges in writing is finding ways to present lots of factual information, about lots of different facts, in a way that keeps readers' interest and doesn't get too confusing.

Using subheadings to let reviewers know you are ending one subject and moving to another can help. The excerpt below is part of the response to the last item in the EPA table above: the environmental or public health concerns facing the community.

EXCERPT...

<u>Local situation</u>: Asthma remains a common, chronic health issue in the St. Louis region. In St. Louis County, the asthma and bronchiolitis hospital admission rate among youth is 402 per 10,000 people. This is greater than the state rate of 385. Mid and North County rates (919 and 869 respectively) are well above state and county rates. Emergency department visits for children in St. Louis County are one and a half times higher in the county than the State of Missouri. A similar pattern is seen with youth rates for asthma. Mid and North County Emergency Department visit rates (1,092 and 2,080, respectively) are markedly higher than county-wide rates.

In this particular example, the focus was on the local community, as the RFA directed. But we emphasized how the situation is worse in the local community than in the state or entire county. This is an effective way to make your case that the need in your community is greater than elsewhere.

That was just one paragraph of a much longer narrative. A federal need section will be chock-full of statistics and data. If you're not careful, all of that data can begin to run together. Often it is easier to present complex need data in tables than to try to explain it in a narrative. A bonus is that tables can take less space to present the same information than it would have taken to write it all out.

The excerpt on the next page was written in response to a different RFA. In this narrative regarding the need for housing for the elderly, we first make our case that there is a high percentage of older residents in our service area. In the excerpt, the table illustrates that there are more elderly residents in the target area than in the county as a whole.

Layering Data Sources to Tell the Whole Story

We often combine multiple sources of data into one need statement. For one recent proposal, we found that the census data were just not painting the picture we needed to tell about the neighborhoods that were going to be reached by our project.

We needed to include the census data to prove the size of the population to be served and to list the poverty rate of the community. Unfortunately, the boundaries of census tracts don't fall neatly along neighborhood lines. In these situations, pockets of need may be hidden within communities that look largely prosperous.

So we also added information about high crime rates that was retrieved from a national online site. We included anecdotal information from high school counselors on the number of homeless students. These additional data sources would not be sufficient if they were all we had, but you can use them to supplement more recognizable sources to make your case stronger. Such alternative sources of need information can be especially useful to you if more traditional data sources seem to mask how dire the situation truly is.

stories from
the real world

Notice that we don't just plunk a table down and expect readers to interpret it the way we want them to. We make sure to point reviewers to the important items in the table and explain how those items contribute to our case for need.

EXCERPT...

As indicated by the table below, the percentage of residents who are 65 years and older in Affton is significantly larger than the rest of St. Louis County.

Age: Affton & St. Louis County 2005 U.S. Census Estimates		
Age Group	Affton	St. Louis County
65 years and older	20.9%	13.4%

Further, Social Security Administration records indicate that approximately 7.8% of households in Affton receive social security benefits—one of the highest percentages of benefit recipients in the Midwest.

Complicating the situation for many seniors living in the community is the fact that generally, Affton's houses are older. Most homes here were built in the 1950s and 1960s. When you stop to consider that the U.S. Census estimates that 75% of Affton's housing is owner-occupied, it is easy to see the burden that seniors face as they age in their own homes.

Good need statements build their story by stacking important facts and by alternating tables with descriptive text. The need statement in the excerpt presents timely factual data with hard numbers, as required. But then it helps paint a picture in readers' minds of an older person living in an old, run-down home and trying to maintain it on a limited income.

Not all tables are as short as the one in the excerpt above. Sometimes tables can contain much more information. Imagine trying to explain the poverty and education rates for eighteen counties at one time! If you take some time to be thoughtful about how you organize complicated data in your tables, they can be powerful tools for communicating a lot of data. But be sure to edit the information or find ways to group and summarize it, or tables can overwhelm your readers as much as a dense narrative.

Explaining Why Current Resources Are Inadequate

Another way to make the case for need in your community is to demonstrate that your community or organization

Some people understand information easily from looking at a table or matrix. Others absorb information better through narrative description. Chances are good that you will have both kinds of people reviewing your grant proposal. Using a mixture of tables and narrative throughout your grant proposal can help you respond to the preferred communications style of all types of reviewers. And that means more points for you.

practical tip

has insufficient resources to solve the problems itself. For example, the excerpt below explains why existing senior housing options are insufficient to meet the need identified in the target community.

EXCERPT...

Unfortunately, the Affton community does not have an existing HUD Section-202 project within the community boundaries. While there are facilities nearby (AHEPA 53, Laclede Manor, St. Joseph Apartments on Cardinal Carberry Campus or Holy Infant Apartments on Cardinal Carberry Campus), each of these facilities operates at or near capacity, with waiting lists. Even the newest facility nearby is, according to the manager, approaching capacity much faster than was anticipated.

The paragraph above serves two purposes. First, it demonstrates that the applicant is knowledgeable about and connected to others providing the same or similar services in the local community. Clearly, the applicants for the senior housing project in the excerpt talked to their "competitors." Second, it makes the case that there remains a gap in services in the community. It accomplishes this by stating that other places where seniors might live are at or near capacity.

RFAs often ask you to demonstrate that your proposed services do not duplicate services already being provided in your community. It is rarely convincing to try to make your case for need by claiming that no one else in the community is doing what you propose to do. Rather, it is much more effective to show that you know what other services are being offered—and then show how your services will be different or that they overcome some other gap.

Where Do I Find the Data I Need?

Finding relevant data is the key to proving need. How do you know where to start?

The answer varies based on what agency you are writing to and what sort of project you are proposing. For example, you would need very different sorts of data for a project to serve low-income elementary students than you would for a flood control project. For education projects, you will likely access the National Center for Education Statistics or your state's department of education. For flood control projects, you will probably access data from the Federal Emergency Management Agency (FEMA), the Army Corps of Engineers, or the Environmental Protection Agency (EPA).

Here is a short list of some of the most commonly cited federal sources of data (for a more complete list, with URLs to each source, consult **Appendix I**):

◆ *US Bureau of the Census*. Population and demographics, along with education levels, poverty, home ownership, primary industries, and so on

◆ *Bureau of Labor Statistics.*
Unemployment rates, productivity,
workplace injuries, and more

◆ *US Department of Labor.* Information
about professions, which are
projected to grow, pay scales,
education needed

◆ *Centers for Disease Control.* Health
issues from Alzheimer's to obesity to
infectious diseases and bioterrorism

◆ *National Center for Education
Statistics (NCES).* For all sorts of
information related to schools,
teachers, students, and graduation
rates up through graduate school

Reviewers will consider the quality of
the sources of the data you use to prove
community need, and they often have
opinions about whether your sources are
current enough to be reliable. Provide
the most current data possible, from
the most reliable sources you can. If
we are concerned that a source may
not look current enough for reviewers,
we sometimes add a note to reviewers
that the information is the most
recent available.

Foundations, research organizations, and industry groups also publish research and white papers on topics of national interest. They are good sources for supplementing the government sources listed above. For example, the Annie E. Casey Foundation collects and publishes data focused on the well-being of children. The Pew Research Center provides information on social issues, attitudes, and trends, including religion, access to technology, and generational issues.

Sometimes federal sources or national-level data either do not have what you need or you need to supplement them. For example, you may need information from your state, county, school district, or local planning district to better illustrate the true local situation. These can include things like health statistics, information about schools and school districts, local employment numbers, and economic development information.

You can also tap resources such as community needs assessments, marketing surveys, white papers, newspaper articles, and local community foundations to support the case for need. Local libraries often have experts in federal documents, including the Census. Get to

Gather and keep current information that tells the story of the community you serve. This usually includes census data on the population, race, median income, poverty rate, and age. Depending on your organization's mission, you may also collect unemployment rates, information on free and reduced rates in the local school district, or local reports, such as those put out by the Area Agency on Aging. Keeping the relevant data in a spreadsheet or other format allows you to update it quickly for future proposals with the most current data. You can also keep a clippings file (online or paper) that collects stories about challenges in your community.

know your local librarians. Chances are if they don't know how to find the information, they know someone who does.

Now that you've laid out the case for the dire need in your community, you get to present the reviewers with the obvious solution: your project.

To Recap

◆ Never, ever assume that your reviewers know anything about your community or its needs.

◆ Keep stacking up the data in support of your need until the case is overwhelming.

◆ The need statement should anticipate your project design, which will be part of the solution.

◆ Don't be afraid to ask for help with finding and understanding data. Your local librarian is a good place to start.

Chapter Ten

Proposal Sections: Project Description

IN THIS CHAPTER

···→ Linking your project to the need

···→ Describing your project clearly and thoroughly

···→ Summarizing your strategies in a work plan

···→ Developing timelines for project activities

You've made your case for need. There are some serious problems in your community or among your target population. Now what are you going to do about it?

In the project description, you get to shine. This is all about your plan. What creative and wonderful ideas do you have to address those needs or problems you have just described?

Strong project narratives convince reviewers that you have planned every detail of your activities: Who will do what when. Where it will happen. What your plan is to overcome possible obstacles. This is your "shark tank," your chance to convince possibly skeptical investors that yours is one of the best ideas from among dozens, perhaps hundreds. Often this section is worth the most points.

Getting Started Writing

If you followed our advice in earlier chapters, you have developed a nice logic model that's a general outline of your project activities. Using the logic model as your guide, you can then begin to fill in more information about each activity.

Sometimes RFAs ask you to explain how your project activities will meet the need but never actually ask you to describe your project. You may decide to provide the reviewers a brief summary of your project before launching into a detailed response to the RFA criteria.

food for thought

Another strategy some writers use to get started on their project description is to brainstorm all of the work they will do if they get the grant. Those items can be converted into grant activities, with details added to flesh out the narrative. Do your brainstorming, and then check the RFA to make sure you have included all of the elements the funding agency is seeking.

For example, the excerpt below contains the instructions for what to include in a project narrative from an actual RFA. As you know from **Chapter Eight**, we recommend that you take all of the points from the list below and make them into subheadings. In fact, we break each of these points into more than one subheading because they contain multiple concepts.

EXCERPT...

Criterion 2: RESPONSE (20 points)

The extent to which:

- The proposed project responds to the "Purpose" included in the funding opportunity description and directly relates with the information presented in the "Needs Assessment" section of the program narrative.
- The proposed activities are capable of addressing the problem and attaining the project objectives.
- The proposed goals and objectives have a clear correlation to addressing the identified need as well as barriers and are measurable, realistic, and achievable in a specific timeframe.

While those three items don't take up much space in the RFA, your response may take up twenty pages of narrative. The good news is that these criteria ask you to tell a story in a pretty coherent fashion. Here is the story outline, using the evaluation criteria as topic sentences for each subheading:

◆ Our project responds to the program purpose in that it...

◆ The proposed program addresses the community need because it directly...

(Did you notice that we split number one into two sections? They are clearly two separate topics.)

◆ The planned activities are capable of addressing the problems identified in the need section for several reasons...

◆ The planned activities will result in reaching the project objectives because...

(Again, the second item was split into two subheadings, as it contains two points that are very different from one another.)

◆ We propose the following goals and objectives…

(Notice we added this bullet. The RFA never actually asks for your goals and objectives. Or they may be requested later in the evaluation criteria. If that's the case, we may preview them here or refer the reader to that section.)

This is a good place to remind you that your first drafts of your logic model and budget were just that—drafts. Once you start writing out project details, you often realize you have to change your original plans. That is a normal part of the ongoing iterative process of project design.

◆ The project goals and objectives relate to the identified need in that…

◆ The proposed goals and objectives are SMART because…

Providing Specific Details

What will set your project narrative apart from everyone else's is telling your project story in clear detail. Even if these questions are never explicitly asked by the RFA, always think in terms of "who, what, when, and where." Providing more detail demonstrates more planning. More planning makes you look good.

For example, compare the following two sentences about an after-school program. Both are true statements about the same program. But the second sentence provides enough information that you understand immediately how this program will work.

◆ Tutors will facilitate after-school learning experiences for at-risk students from XYZ Elementary School.

◆ At least thirty at-risk third-grade students from XYZ Elementary School will receive tutoring and homework assistance from qualified tutors for fifty minutes per day, five days per week, in the school's library.

A bonus is that the second sentence starts right off with the recipients of your program and what they will receive or experience. It is more focused on those you serve. The first example's emphasis is on your personnel and what they will do. It's more internally focused.

All of this detail is great. In the example in our text, we say how many students receive how many contact hours. Don't forget, though, that if you change your project activities, there is usually a budget impact. Similarly, if you have to cut your budget to serve fewer people or reduce tutoring sessions, remember to update the project description so it still matches the budget.

Linking Your Plan to the Need

The excerpt from the RFA above asks you to describe how your project responds directly to the needs you described earlier in your narrative. This linkage between the project activities and the need goes both ways. Sometimes, as your project develops, you actually need to go back and add a new point to your need section so the two sections are parallel.

Come right out and tell reviewers how what you are doing is the logical solution to the problems in the community that you have described. Connect the dots for your readers.

important

Not all RFAs come right out and ask for this information clearly. But make sure you find a way to weave an explanation of this linkage into your narrative anyway.

Let's say you are working from a community needs assessment that revealed the following needs or problems in the service area:

◆ A high number of students are at risk of academic failure.

◆ Young people need a safe place to go after school.

◆ The schools can't afford to provide tutoring.

◆ Many parents/caregivers do not know how to encourage or assist their children in completing homework.

If you spent several pages in your need section explaining and proving each of these points, readers will be expecting to see some sort of after-school program that provides tutoring and engages the parents. If serving parents is not included in your activity plan, then do not waste valuable pages describing the situation with parents. You will only set up readers' expectations to see a program element you aren't planning to provide.

Show and Tell

Another way to make your project description stand out from all of the others is to be strategic in how you present your information. Let's be honest, trying to explain all of the details of how your three- or five-year project is going to be implemented, who is going to do what when, can get a little cumbersome. Don't make reviewers wade through twenty pages of unrelenting text.

Take a step back from your project description once you've got it written out. Even better, hand it to someone who is not involved in the project planning. Ask that person: "Is this clear? Can you understand what we are proposing to do? What could we do to make this clearer?"

You may need to go back and add introductory text between subheadings to help connect the dots from section to section. Another effective strategy is to use tables for presenting some of

---

Make Sure the Project Design Links Directly to the Need

Cheryl once worked with a college wanting to add an Upward Bound program. Upward Bound programs provide extra academic assistance and college preparation services to high school students. While the college was situated on the edge of a major metropolitan area, its program would target students farther away from the city, in a rural, high-poverty area. As Cheryl and the client were building the case for need where the students lived, college personnel provided data on the vast service area. Although there was limited public transportation, it took students four hours to travel to the college campus using the public bus system.

Unfortunately, the budget for the program was extremely tight, and the college needed to prioritize other, required, expenses over transportation costs. So we had built a case for the need for transportation, but there would be no transportation provided in the budget. There were two options. They could go back to the need section to delete the section on students' need for transportation, or they would have to find a way to transport students.

In the end, program staff were able to convince the college to commit to transporting students at its own expense, using college vehicles. But if they had been unable to find a solution, they would have had to cut the discussion of rural service area and the barriers students would face in trying to participate in the program from the need section.

stories from
the real world

---

your plan. Don't overdo it, but tables can break up long sections of text that can overwhelm your reader.

Tables can force you to get organized. We like them because they can be effective at summarizing complex information for a reviewer, making that information easier to understand than trying to narrate each step in writing. The following excerpt is a portion of a table that we used to respond to a requirement to describe our plan for communicating with several required stakeholder groups and recruiting high school students into an after-school program.

Notice, however, that we don't just drop the table in with no context. We like to guide the readers and tell them what the table says.

EXCERPT...

(1) Plan to Inform Faculty and Staff and Others in the Target Area of the Goals and Objectives of the Project. The plan to inform others of the proposed project uses a variety of communication strategies to ensure that faculty and staff, target school personnel, partners, students, parents, and the general public are aware of the project. The specific communication plan is outlined in the following table.

EXCERPT...

Plan to Inform Others of Goals and Objectives of Proposed Project		
Target Audience	Timeline	Action Steps
Applicant Faculty and Staff	Immediately upon Award Notification	Email to all faculty/staff from Project Director announcing project
	Within 1 Month of Award Notification	Announcement of project at first faculty meeting after award notice
	Ongoing	Develop and maintain a project website with information about project purpose, objectives, services, and eligibility requirements
Target School Personnel	Immediately upon Award Notification	Request placement on next school board meeting agenda to inform board of project

Project Director contacts principals to request opportunity to speak at next staff meeting |
| | Within 1 Month of Award Notification | Letter to high school counselors with project goals, objectives, and a request for help in identifying potential participants |
| | Ongoing | Annual meeting with counselors to inform them of program and deliver information packets

Annual orientation session with faculty/staff |

This table condensed several double-spaced pages that were hard to follow into one page of easy-to-understand content. The actual table in the proposal contained several additional rows of activities to take place with three more target audiences. This type of information is a good candidate for putting into table form.

What Makes a Plan a Plan

Many federal agencies will ask you to provide a work plan—possibly as part of your project description or maybe as an attachment. A work plan is a detailed description (usually in the form of a table or matrix) that outlines the who, what, when, and where of your program. You may think you've already covered that. The advice we have given all along in this chapter is to be specific, say who will do what, and give details about how and when things will happen. All of this contributes to assuring readers that you have a real plan and not just a vague idea.

Some guidelines allow applicants to use single-spaced text in tables and charts, even when the narrative is required to be double-spaced. Check the RFA to see if that is allowed for your application. Double-spaced tables save very little space and can be harder to read than straight narrative. However, single-spaced tables can be extremely helpful if you are struggling to come in under the page limit.

 practical tip

If you have already done this, taking the same information and putting it into a table or chart should not take you too much time. If you have not thought your activities through to that level of detail, then the work plan gives you that extra push you might need. Work plans are especially important for multiyear projects, since you may have different major activities taking place in different years.

What makes a plan stand out from a simple list of activities is that for something to count as a "plan," it usually must include information such as who is responsible for each activity and when that activity will occur. In the case of a multipartner consortium, your plans may demonstrate whose resources are being used to accomplish which activities.

If your RFA does not prescribe the format of your work plan, you have a lot of flexibility in how you present yours. If your project is not too complex, your work plan may be simply written narrative, perhaps bullets. Most often, though, such plans appear in a matrix or table. Personally, we prefer the RFA tell us how to format our plan. That way we are more confident our plan will meet reviewer expectations.

Consider this next excerpt. We always have to chuckle when we read this federal agency's "suggestion" about how you may wish to organize your work plan. We have underlined a few words to show you what we mean.

> Work plans and logic models can both be described as being a snapshot or quick overview of your project, but they are different. A logic model is designed to show how your activities will produce certain outcomes and impacts. A work plan really digs down into all of your activities to describe how they will take place.

important

EXCERPT...

"The applicant describes a clear and coherent workplan that is aligned with the project's goals and objectives. <u>This may be presented as a matrix</u> that illustrates the project goals, strategies, activities, and measurable process and outcome measures in a quick reference format. The workplan must outline the **individual or organization responsible** for carrying out each activity and **include a timeline** for all three years of the grant. The workplan for the second and third year of the grant may be somewhat less detailed."

Remember how we said that you should always take all of a funding agency's "suggestions"? Despite the tentative words, we took these instructions seriously and designed a matrix with a column for each major item listed in the RFA text. Our one concession was to put the goal outside the table, because there just was no room otherwise. However, the goal and the subsequent objectives are very clear. The excerpt below contains just a few rows from a work plan that was developed in response to that RFA. Any acronyms used in the work plan were explained in the narrative previously if they were not defined in the work plan itself.

EXCERPT...

Goal #1: Increase Access to Health Care

Objective 1.1: Increase access for the uninsured and medically underserved

Strategy	Activities	Outcomes & Measurement	Performance Period	Responsible Parties
Position X Clinic to become a Federally-Qualified Health Center (FQHC)	1. Apply for FQHC Look Alike status	1. Completed Look Alike application	1. Dec 08	1. Clinic & Tech. Writer
	2. Research & coordinate with existing FQHCs	2. Information to prepare application	2. Jun 08	2. Network Director and Clinic
	3. Conduct research to complete instrument	3. Adequate data for NFA	3. May 08 - Jun 09	3. Net. Dir., Researchers
	4. Coordinate with SORH to complete required NFA	4. Completed NFA; eligible score	4. Jul 09	4. Net. Dir., Tech. Writer

For each activity, the table states how that activity will be measured or what we expect the outcome to be. The table also includes dates for completion or a period during which activities will take place. Finally, the last column lists the person, organization, or team responsible for each activity. Notice we used position titles rather than the names of individuals. The individuals who hold positions can change, but positions are usually pretty stable.

Timelines

In the case of the prior example, the timeline was considered to have been included in the work plan. However, sometimes you are asked to provide a stand-alone timeline. Whatever format one takes, a timeline indicates when important activities will take place and when certain milestones will be reached.

Timelines demonstrate that you can realistically accomplish all of your planned activities within the limited project period. They are also very helpful for projects that have dependencies, like construction projects. A dependency is when Activity B can't take place until Activity A is complete. So you can't break ground on your new building (Activity B) until you have received all of your permits (Activity A). Finally,

The annotated complete proposals in *Writing to Win Federal Grants–The Workbook* include work plans you can use as models.

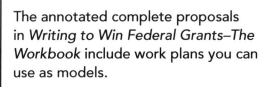

The Workbook

Find Good Models to Follow

Karen remembers the first time she had to create a timeline. It did not go well. It was only her second federal proposal ever, and the RFA required a timeline.

She remembers scratching her head, thinking she had no idea what a "timeline" looked like. It didn't help that this was in pre-word processor days. This was during typewriter days. No easy way to make tables, and no handy tools to make graphics like flowcharts or boxes with text in them.

Having no models to go on, she did the best she could and wrote out her timeline in a narrative format. Sadly, her proposal did not get funded. When she obtained the reviewer comments, one jumped out at her: "The timeline was not clear."

Never one to be shy, Karen called up the program officer to ask what she should do in the future to make her timelines easier to follow. He went on to describe how most applicants purchased graph paper, wrote their timelines on the graph paper, and then taped the graph paper into their narrative.

It's a wonder that alone didn't send her screaming from federal proposals. Fortunately, we have better tools at our disposal today and lots of good models to follow.

stories from the real world

a detailed timeline is another element that convinces reviewers that you have done your homework and planned your project thoroughly.

There are really no rules for what timelines should look like. They can take many different forms, from a simple bulleted list to a table. If there are no instructions in your RFA that indicate a preferred format, use your best judgment regarding the most effective way to present your timeline. The simplest type of timeline just presents your project chronologically.

The project for which the timeline in the next excerpt was created fit a chronological organization nicely. Certain activities would take place at the beginning of the semester. There were quarterly parent nights, with a different topic addressed at each meeting. The excerpt omits the final month of the timeline, but we almost always make sure to include any evaluation activities and final reports in real timelines.

EXCERPT...	
Project Timeline	
Month	Tasks to be Accomplished and Milestones
July 2009	• Grant Project Period Begins
August	• Staff and volunteers recruited and trained • Centers stocked/prepared for new school year

EXCERPT...

Project Timeline	
Month	Tasks to be Accomplished and Milestones
September	• Children referred to and enrolled at Learning Centers • Entrance interviews held and Personal Success Plans developed • Academic assistance and enrichment begin (continue monthly) • Parent Night—Project orientation • Annual Performance Review (APR) submitted to state Dept. of Ed.
October	• Parent Night—Exercise & Learning • Project Director attends fall Project Directors' meeting • First field trip
November	• Parent Night—Positive Behavior Management

However, not all projects follow such a clear chronological series of steps. When we sat down to start the timeline that appears in the next excerpt, we started trying a traditional month-to-month format. It just didn't work. The project for which the second timeline was created had several important activities that happen more than once during a year or that are ongoing.

Listing each activity out by month required a lot of repetition. In this instance, it took less space to organize major activities in rows and check off the month in which that activity would take place. The actual table was longer than the excerpt below, as there were more activities during the year, but we included representative rows to illustrate different sorts of activities. Notice that this table includes rows for evaluation tasks, reinforcing the quality of our evaluation plan. This timeline clearly shows that we have a schedule to accomplish all planned activities.

EXCERPT...

State College Annual Project Timeline												
	Month											
Critical Element	Sep	Oct	Nov	Dec	Jan	Feb	Mar	Apr	May	Jun	Jul	Aug
Recruit, Hire and Train Staff								x	x	x	x	
Identify New Participants	x	x	x	x	x	x	x	x	x	x	x	x
Select New Participants	x				x							x
Needs Assessments	x				x							
Reconcile Budget	x	x	x	x	x	x	x	x	x	x	x	x
Formative Evaluation	x	x	x	x	x	x	x	x	x	x	x	x
Summative Evaluation					x				x			x

Putting content into a table does not automatically mean the content will be easy to read. We have seen some convoluted tables in our day. That is why we keep encouraging you to leave yourself plenty of time to approach all aspects of your program description strategically. In the case of the second timeline, we decided it was easier for reviewers to read if we "flipped" the rows and columns.

Look at each subheading of your proposal with a critical eye and ask yourself if you have made the information in that section as clear as possible. Show your tables to people not on your grants team to be sure they can interpret what you are trying to communicate. That extra attention to clarity and detail will help you earn every single possible point for your project design section.

To Recap

◆ The project description is one of the most important sections of your narrative.

◆ Whether you are required to include work plans, timelines, or just narrative, the goal is to prove that you have planned your project in incredible detail. You have thought of everything.

◆ Tell your readers; then show them. Never insert a table or chart without telling readers what you want them to derive from that illustration.

Chapter Eleven

Proposal Sections: Goals and Objectives

IN THIS CHAPTER

- ···→ Goals and objectives the federal way

- ···→ Different types of objectives

- ···→ Writing SMART objectives

It's time to break out that logic model again. Now you are really going to put it to use. In your project description, you focused on the details of the activities you will undertake with the grant funds. Now we are going to talk about what those activities actually help you accomplish. What has changed because of your grant project? Is water cleaner? Are children's grades improving? Do senior citizens have safe, affordable housing?

Something big and visionary and bold should be your project's goal. Objectives are the steps you take along the way to reaching your goal. You usually have to be able to measure objectives. How many steps were there? How long was each stride? Did we take as many steps as we said we would?

Describing goals and objectives this way is how it usually works. However, not every funding agency got the memo or went to the same workshop we did. In reality, the people who write the funding notice may know less about goals and objectives than you do. They may call something an objective that you know is really a goal. They may tell you to write measurable objectives, but then the models they give you to follow aren't all that measurable.

Just be flexible and be ready to adapt to whatever standards and terminology your funding agency uses.

Goals

Goals are big-picture, long-term statements. They might even sound like your mission statement. It is usually not possible to fully achieve the goals you present in your proposal within the time frame of a grant-funded project.

In fact, your project goal could easily be on your organization's list for years, through multiple grant-funded projects.

For example, some organizations have goals like these in their strategic plan, or they may write goals like these for a grant-funded project:

Goal: A statement of a desired big-picture outcome or long-term effect on the community or world.

Objective: A specific and measurable result of a single program or project. Objectives are measurable ways to make progress toward achieving our greater goals.

◆ Reduce hospital readmissions for cardiac patients.

◆ Increase the number of students who earn bachelor's degrees within four years of enrolling.

◆ Improve financial literacy and stability among the immigrant population.

Think about it this way. You can always continue to "reduce" or "increase" or "improve." You will never quite arrive at such a goal. There is always room for continued improvement (which means room for many grant-funded projects over the years). Your three-year project may successfully increase the number of students earning bachelor's degrees within four years (down from six years, which is the standard measure). Even so, you will no doubt want to continue to improve graduation rates. Likewise, will you ever completely conquer cardiovascular disease in your community? You can keep targeting such a goal, chipping away at it for years. Decades even.

If you are drawing goals from an existing strategic plan, you may have to work with goals that are less than perfect. Don't be afraid to edit when necessary. However, if nothing in the strategic plan matches up with your planned project, think carefully about whether you are departing from your mission.

Objectives

In contrast, objectives are usually finite and completed by the end of the grant. You may have several objectives that all contribute to one goal. For example, if your goal is to improve financial literacy and stability among the immigrant population in your service area, one grant objective could be stated: "Up to 75 percent of immigrants attending financial literacy courses will have opened and contributed to a savings account eight months after the courses."

Until every immigrant in your community has been reached with financial literacy classes, you could continue to recycle this objective, changing the date. Notice that this objective proposes to measure success by the number of class participants who open savings accounts (an outcome). It goes beyond merely counting how many people came to class (which is merely an output).

It can help to approach writing your objectives from the perspective of your grant-funded activities. Ask yourself: "If we teach financial literacy classes, what do we want the result to be?" The question is always the same, no matter what the activity: "If we do [fill-in-the blank], what are we hoping to achieve?"

Make it your mission to create SMART objectives:

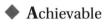 **S**pecific

 Measurable

 Achievable

 Realistic

 Time limited

Make your objectives as specific as possible, without making them too long. And be specific about something that can be measured. In the example above, it is possible to measure the percentage of students who attended our class who report that they are using a savings account when we ask them eight months later.

> Make sure that your objectives are reasonable and that you will be able to measure them. It is very common to come back to your draft objectives and revise them once you have written the evaluation plan and determined exactly what you can and cannot measure as well as what tool(s) you will need for doing the measuring.
>
>

It is usually not enough for an objective to merely state that stream pollution will decrease. Whenever possible, state by how much it will decrease. Then make sure to set a target that is reasonable for you to achieve within your budget and the grant period. You could say pollution will decrease by 75 percent. That's definitely measurable. But is it realistic? Could you really achieve that by the end of your one-year grant? Maybe you can, but it would be a good idea to explain to your reviewers why you are confident your target is doable.

> We've probably all fallen into the trap of mistaking activities for objectives. When you are asked to state your project's objectives, it's pretty easy to say something like "offer tutoring" or "teach savings classes" or "provide books." We immediately begin to think about the things we are going to *do*. If you stay focused on the results of what you do, that will help you create strong objectives.
>
>

Good objectives strike a balance between being ambitious and visionary and being achievable.

Process Objectives and Outcome Objectives

In an ideal world, we all write measurable, achievable outcome objectives. However, reality often intrudes. It does no good to write wonderful-sounding outcome objectives if you are unable to measure and report on your promised outcomes. Your goals and objectives are intimately tied to your evaluation plan. The evaluation budget or our own internal capacity to conduct evaluation often forces us to scale back our objectives. It may just be too expensive to try to measure outcomes. Or perhaps long-

Process objective: An objective that states that an activity or something will get "done," such as a certain number of students attending tutoring sessions. Things achieved if we accomplish process objectives are referred to as "outputs."

Outcome objective: An objective that states the change that occurs in people or the community as a result of the activity taking place. For example, demonstrating that students increased their learning because they were tutored. Things achieved if we accomplish outcome objectives are called "outcomes."

term outcomes won't occur until after the grant period ends and your report is due.

Sometimes you will just not be comfortable predicting an outcome. This may be because you are implementing a new program in which you have no experience. Or it may be that you are afraid of predicting an outcome and then failing to achieve it. Whatever the reason, we often find ourselves falling back on what are called "process objectives." Process objectives measure outputs. They prove that you reached a certain number of people or completed a certain activity.

For example, consider the two objectives in the excerpt below. Objective 1 is a process objective. It merely states how many people will be reached with the educational message. Objectives 2 and 3 are outcome objectives.

Objective 2 predicts that the number of students with an unhealthy body mass index (BMI) will decrease. However, we should point out that this objective would be even stronger if the applicant had felt confident or knowledgeable enough to predict what percentage of students would achieve a healthy BMI.

Objective 3 predicts that the members of this consortium will demonstrate increased collaboration. Again, this objective falls short of stating how much collaboration will increase. But it does explain how we will know collaboration has increased: We will administer an instrument that measures collaboration among partners. The instrument will be administered at the beginning of the relationship and again at the end of the grant period ("pre" and "post").

EXCERPT...

Objective 1: By the end of the three-year project period, reach at least 5,100 youth and adults in the target population with the *5-2-1-0 Let's Go* message. [process objective]

Objective 2: Among school-aged youth who are advised to adopt a Healthy Weight Plan, decrease the percent whose BMI is outside the healthy range. [outcome objective – lacking a performance target]

Objective 3: By the end of the project period, coalition members will demonstrate increased collaboration among themselves, based on pre-and post-measures of collaborative activities. [outcome objective – giving how outcome will be measured – but lacking a performance target]

In the end, these three objectives were considered sufficient and this project was funded. We suspect that even though these objectives were far from perfect, many applicants probably had no outcome objectives at all.

The lesson is that if you can squeeze even one outcome objective out of a list of three to four process objectives, you may stand out above your competition. But don't count on it. Make all your objectives as outcome oriented as possible.

Test Yourself

Two of the sample goals offered at the beginning of this chapter are listed here again, along with the actual objectives that were written for their respective grant projects. Determine for yourself which objectives are outcome objectives and which are process objectives:

◆ Goal: Reduce hospital readmissions for cardiac patients.

◆ Objective: 100 percent of cardiac care team members will be trained to assess patients at high risk for readmission.

◆ Objective: Hospital readmission rates will decrease 30 percent over baseline by year three.

◆ Objective: By year three, 60 percent of patients will make and complete follow-up care visits as indicated on discharge orders .

And these are from a completely different project:

◆ Goal: Increase the number of students earning bachelor's degrees within four years.

◆ Objective: By June 30, 20xx, implement an "early alert" system for notifying advisors when students are in danger of failing classes.

◆ Objective: By December 31, 20xx, 80 percent of students referred to tutoring will increase their GPA by one-quarter percentage point.

◆ Objective: By the end of year five [of the project], the number of freshmen who return as sophomores will increase from a baseline of 70 percent to 78 percent.

Setting Performance Targets for Objectives

The outcome objectives had numbers associated with them, such as "increase the number of freshmen who return as sophomores from 70 percent to 78 percent" or "hospital readmission rates will decrease by 30 percent from the baseline."

These numbers that you are expected to achieve are called performance targets. Your "target" for freshman-to-sophomore retention is 78 percent. Is that the right number? How do you know?

In the case of the retention scenario, we provided you with an important clue. You received the "baseline number." The baseline is a measure of what is being achieved now. You know that before you deliver any tutoring or implement a first-year experience program, 70 percent of freshmen return as sophomores. You are claiming that after students receive your services, this retention rate will climb to 78 percent.

Performance target: A number that appears in specific, measurable objectives that will have to be achieved by the end of the grant period.

Baseline: A number that indicates the rate at which something is happening now, before you deliver your program services.

How do you settle on 78 percent instead of 80 or 72 percent? Talk to your colleagues who did this at another institution. Find an expert in the field. Do research. In this particular example, first-year experiences are not groundbreaking. We could expect to find journal articles about success rates of other programs.

Whatever process you use to set an achievable performance target, it's a good idea to explain that process to your reviewers. One reviewer might think that a gain of eight percentage points is unrealistically high. Another might consider it too cautious. We have actually received comments back from reviewers of the same proposal who did not agree among themselves whether the target set in our objective was ambitious or underachieving.

In the case of the financial literacy objective discussed at the beginning of this chapter, it did not include a baseline. It would be ideal and wonderful if you could measure participant knowledge before class and after class. But it's probably not required.

The most important thing is to set your performance targets thoughtfully. You are making educated guesses. There may be extenuating factors in your community that will affect how achievable your targets are. If so, explain them briefly. You should have a reason for the target you set, and you should be able to discuss why that target is ambitious yet attainable within the timeframe of the grant project.

Putting It All Together

You may be wondering, "how many of these goals and objectives do I need?"

The answer is, "it depends."

It depends on the requirements of the RFA. It depends on the nature of your project. It depends on how big the grant budget is and how long the grant period is. And it depends on the funding agency. Some agencies must have been tired of receiving poorly written objectives, because they tell the applicants what their objectives will be.

For example, the US Department of Education often provides prewritten objectives that every applicant must use. All you have to do is fill in the appropriate performance target for your program. There are no goals. Some Housing and Urban Development (HUD) programs even force applicants to select from drop-down menus.

If there is no requirement for a certain number of goals and/or objectives for your project, it is usually simpler to keep the list short. The fewer the objectives, the less you will have to measure during evaluation. Too many objectives can make a proposal confusing to follow.

To Recap

- ◆ Focus on outcomes when writing objectives.

- ◆ Set achievable performance targets based on your knowledge of what can be achieved.

- ◆ We sometimes have to settle for process objectives, but try to include at least one outcome objective when possible.

Chapter Twelve

Proposal Sections: Organizational Capacity and Quality

IN THIS CHAPTER

- ···➤ Demonstrating the applicant has adequate resources to implement the project

- ···➤ Presenting the applicant's experience/expertise at managing and delivering projects

- ···➤ Explaining what personnel will be needed to run the project

- ···➤ Showing that existing or to-be-hired personnel will have the needed qualifications and expertise to run the project

This chapter is a fun one, because it's all about you. Your mother may have taught you that it is impolite to brag. You may not be comfortable tooting your own horn. But in this context, it's good to brag.

Most federal proposals ask applicants to address "organizational capacity" in some way. Whatever they call it, the funder's goal is the same—to find out which applicants are the best bet. With which one of you will they invest their money? They are taking a risk on you, usually sight unseen. They are looking for assurances that you won't make them look bad by misusing their funds or failing to complete your project.

You may see questions about your ability to properly manage and track grant funds. Or they may ask you to describe the skills and experience of your personnel. You might need to describe your track record of implementing similar projects or working with similar populations.

Definitely provide the facts in your answers. But also seize every opportunity to portray your organization as more than competent. You want reviewers and agency staff to come away from your proposal convinced that your organization is the perfect fit. That you are among the best at what you do. That you are obviously someone to call on when things need to get done. That they should give money to *you*.

Recognizing Organizational Capacity Questions in the RFA

Not all RFAs will come right out and say they are asking about organizational capacity. This is a catch-all term we are using that includes responses to some or all of the following common prompts or questions found in federal RFAs:

> Don't get hung up on titles. An RFA may not call the items we're covering in this chapter "organizational capacity." In most cases, you will be called upon to address some or all of the concepts we group together here, even if they are spread out within the RFA or called something different.

◆ How many years have you been serving people in the target service area?

◆ How many years have you delivered the same or similar services?

◆ What existing relationships do you have in the target service area?

◆ How much space or other resources (like computers) are available to deliver the necessary services?

◆ How much experience do you have at administering and accounting for federal funds?

◆ What evidence can you provide of adequate fiscal controls?

◆ What management policies and procedures are in place to ensure this project will be implemented properly?

◆ Have you clearly defined the roles and responsibilities of any partners?

◆ How will you sustain project activities after the grant has ended?

We hope you have already been thinking about the answers to some of these questions, because they parallel the capacity and resources we said you needed to have to be ready to apply for federal grants back in **Chapter Two**.

Regardless of how the questions are worded or what content they cover, your goal is the same: Make clear that your organization is a top-notch organization, with lots of experience and expertise that make it an excellent choice to receive federal funds. The most common types of RFA prompts you will be responding to fall into four categories: resources, management procedures, financial practices, and quality of personnel.

Resources

In this context, resources refers to things such as space, vehicles, supplies, major equipment, or technology. These are things your organization already has or can get access to. They demonstrate that you will be able to get the job done, because you have everything needed that's not covered by the grant budget. They also refer to the financial resources to sustain project activities after the grant ends or your plan to generate these resources.

Sometimes you detail your resources to satisfy an RFA requirement that you demonstrate your organization's "commitment" to a project. Even if matching funds are not required, often applicants who can commit the most resources to support a project receive more points. The value of the resources that you can set aside to support a project is also sometimes called "leverage." Leverage lets funders claim to get more for their grant dollars.

> ### Success Breeds Success
>
> Sometimes people fear that if they make their organization sound too successful, the organization won't look like it needs a grant. Not so. The funding agency is interested only in your community's need for whatever your grant will provide. The funder has no interest in what your organization needs. Actually, the strongest organizations are the ones most likely to win federal grants.
>
> There are a few exceptions to this principle, such as grants for capacity building like Title III and Title V grants available to institutions of higher education. But unless your RFA explicitly asks about your organization's weaknesses or problems, emphasize your strengths, financial stability, and qualified personnel.
>
>

Space

No, we don't mean the final frontier that the Starship Enterprise was heading off to. This is a little more mundane. This is simply about what room you have to deliver your proposed services. Do you have office space for new staff or a hygienic place to deliver inoculations? Can you say that your facilities are accessible to clients with disabilities? If you are fully compliant with the Americans with Disabilities Act (ADA), say so.

If you are going to tutor students after school, where will this take place? Will the school keep a classroom open for you after hours? Will you meet in a community center or a church basement? Any one of these is fine, as long as reviewers are assured you have thought of this detail if it is relevant to your program.

Vehicles or Transportation

Transportation isn't relevant to all projects, but it can be a deal breaker in others. If you are tutoring children after school, how do they get to where this tutoring happens? How do they get home afterward? If you are delivering meals to the homebound, make clear how the deliveries will happen. Whether your organization pays staff to drive its company vehicles or volunteers use their personal cars, explain that you have the resources to ensure the meals will get delivered.

Try to anticipate reviewers' questions. Look at your budget and your project description. Is there something essential to your project's success that's not included in the budget? Maybe you already have that item. Maybe a partner will donate it. Whatever the solution is, find a good place to explain it. Sections like capacity, organizational commitment, or resources are often the best place. But, if there is just no good way to weave that information into the project narrative, we sometimes resort to putting a short note in the budget narrative.

practical tip

Let's be clear. If you have already covered all of these details in the grant budget because van rental, mileage, and wages of the drivers are all allowable expenses, you probably don't have to go into more detail. We are talking here about strategies to describe things that you bring to the table to support project activities that are not included in your budget request.

Supplies, Major Equipment, and Hardware/Software

Similarly, it's often a good idea to describe your equipment or technology capacity to let reviewers know you can complete your planned activities. For example, if your project will provide dental services, explain that you own the digital x-ray machine so reviewers won't wonder whether x-rays will be part of your patient exams. In educational projects, you might need to list what classroom or lab facilities your program will be allowed to use or promise that high school students will be allowed access to the college library.

Just as you need to paint a picture of your need, also paint a picture of how the equipment you or your partners have makes your program feasible.

If you will provide career services to veterans, you may need to say how many computers you have or describe your Internet connection. This would assure reviewers that your program participants will be able to go online to complete their job applications and send their resumes to prospective employers.

Focus on what's logical. What might reviewers wonder about after they read your project description and review the budget?

Management Procedures

The resources section is about what you have. If you are asked to describe your management procedures, that's about how you run your

A program officer once told Karen that one of the primary reasons her proposal for literacy services was funded was because of the detailed descriptions of essential materials and space.

In this case, the proposal described a computer lab, workstations, and space for one-on-one tutoring. Instead of just saying that a computer lab was available, the proposal gave details. There were fifty workstations. Each workstation had a computer that would be preloaded with the curriculum, headphones, and a microphone. The headphones and microphone allowed participants to practice skills essential to improving their reading ability.

stories from the real world

organization. The funder wants assurances that someone in senior leadership (the executive director, the president, or a vice president) will be closely monitoring the grant project and will hold the grant staff accountable.

If the RFA does not ask for specific information, explain as many of the following items that you have space to discuss if they are relevant to your project (financial management issues are addressed in the next section):

◆ Who supervises the project director

◆ How much time the project director will devote to the project (usually discussed in terms of percentage of effort)

◆ How the project director will supervise grant staff, including frequency of meetings

> *Project director*: The most commonly used term to describe the person who is in charge of implementing the grant-funded activities once the grant is awarded. This person is also sometimes called the "principal investigator" or PI.
>
>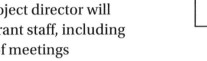

◆ An assurance that the applicant has sound policies for recruiting, hiring, and evaluating staff that will be followed when hiring grant staff

◆ What reports will be produced when and who will receive them

◆ The procedures in place to keep confidential records secure

◆ How equipment purchased with grant funds will be inventoried

◆ Whether an external evaluator will review the project

> If the explanation of who reports to whom on your grant project starts getting convoluted, consider inserting an organizational chart. A concise org chart can make it easy to see which personnel are assigned to your grant project and what the supervisory structure is. Sometimes you are even required to insert these charts.
>
>

Sustainability

Some RFAs will ask applicants to discuss sustainability. This is usually the funding agency's way of asking organizations to discuss how they will continue to sustain the grant-funded activities once the grant period ends. For some reason, this section unnecessarily stresses many grant applicants.

How to best respond to this section depends on the type of project the grant is funding. For example, if the grant is funding construction or renovation of a facility, it will be much less costly to maintain that facility than it was to build or renovate it originally. Once the grant period ends, all you have to do is keep the facility in working order. But what are your plans to

See the annotated full proposals in *Writing to Win Federal Grants–The Workbook* for sample sustainability sections. All of the proposals contained in the workbook received funding.

The Workbook

do that? Where will the money come from? Depending on the size and nature of your organization, the funds to maintain the facility may come from a maintenance endowment, user fees, taxes, or the annual operating budget.

For program grants, grant applicants sometimes argue that implementing changes or activities funded by the grant will result in cost savings (such as energy efficiencies) or increased revenue (such as increased tuition earned because fewer students drop out as a result of the services they are offered). In the latter example, we sometimes speak of grant-funded activities being "institutionalized." The argument you make in your grant proposal is usually that once a program has been proven successful with a few years of data behind it, the organization's leadership will be convinced of the value of program activities and will budget for them accordingly in the future.

A third approach is to point reviewers to the organization's long history of fundraising success from multiple sources and to say that the organization will continue to seek grants and other funds to sustain the project once the federal funds have ended. Be as specific about past successes and possible future opportunities as you can. For your organization's sake, it may be wise to have preliminary conversations with some of your regular foundation or individual supporters to determine if there is interest and ability there to help you sustain program activities after a grant ends.

While it is fine to be honest and say that if no other funds can be obtained, services may have to be cut back once federal funds end, do all you can to minimize that possibility.

Here's what you have to understand about sustainability. The funding agency is not going to check up on you after the fact to see if your sustainability plans worked out. What you say in the sustainability section should be as honest and truthful as it can be when predicting something that far in the future, with many variables affecting its ultimate success. But if all of your sustainability strategies fail, you will not have to pay back your grant. In some instances, it may not even hurt your chances for future funding.

Financial Management Practices

You've seen those news stories too. Someone is heading to jail or paying a fine for misusing

If your organization is relatively new to government grants, it will be especially important for you to explain that your qualified financial staff are knowledgeable about federal regulations. Describe your policies for ensuring that any expenditures are documented and charged to the appropriate account. Explain how you will educate program staff about the grant budget and how the budget must guide their expenditures.

important

After you get the grant, give a copy of the detailed budget and budget narrative to your finance or business office. Call a meeting with the project's staff and share the budget with them too (you may need to hide salaries). Be as transparent as possible. Everyone needs to know that the grant budget is a contract. Grant funds can be spent only on things that are in the grant budget, on pain of death.

grant funds. It never ceases to amaze us how a few people seem to think that grants are their own personal expense accounts. Of course, you know better.

Understandably, federal agencies and Congress are worried about fraud. As a result, more and more RFAs are asking you to explain how you will ensure that grant funds are spent properly. What fiscal controls are in place? Who is checking up on the project director and the budget?

The first time you write a federal grant, you may not know most of this information. When you start asking questions, that may even prompt your organization to revise or tighten up some of its policies. That's great. Here are the sorts of things you might need to explain in a section on financial management practices:

◆ Purchasing procedures (such as requiring an invoice or purchase order) before making payment

◆ Who approves expenditures and the process for ensuring expenditures are appropriate

◆ Staff reimbursement policies

◆ Travel policies, especially regarding international travel, if relevant

◆ Process of obtaining competitive bids, if required by the agency or RFA

◆ Who manages the grant "books"

◆ How often the project director reviews the financial records and how often someone over the project director reviews the books

◆ Whether your financial records are regularly audited and whether your audit is an A-133 audit (your auditor can tell you)

A-133 audit: A standard set of financial audit requirements that used to be based on OMB Circular A-133. (Most previous OMB circulars that contained cost principals and audit requirements have been moved to Title 2 of the Code of Federal Regulations and superseded by the "Uniform Administrative Requirements, Cost Principles, and Audit Requirements for Federal Awards" at the *Federal Register*.) For grant awards made on or after December 26, 2014, organizations receiving $750,000 or more in federal funds annually must complete A-133 audits using external auditors. The previous OMB A-133 threshold of $500,000 applied until December 26, 2014. The easiest way to access the most current regulations is to visit federalregister.gov and search for "uniform administrative requirements" (using the quotation marks).

We have provided two brief excerpts below that address some financial management issues. The first excerpt is drawn from a large organization with its own finance department and multiple grants under management at any one time. This applicant was depending on its long track record of successfully managing grants to help prove it has adequate fiscal controls. We were constrained by space to keep the explanation short.

EXCERPT...

Required Evidence of Accurate Accounting Procedures and Appropriate Use of Grant Funds
[The applicant] has more than 30 years of experience implementing federal, state and local grants under a rigorous set of accounting procedures and controls to ensure that funds are properly accounted for. A robust accounting system requires formal processes for authorization of expenditures. A 2008 review of [latest project] by the [X state] Department of Education found our program in full compliance with spending rules. We also have an annual A-133 audit.

In contrast to the large organization discussed in the first excerpt, the second excerpt below was written for a small organization with only three staff. There was no finance department to fall back on—only an office manager with off-the-shelf bookkeeping software. That partly explains why this excerpt makes a point to describe how the separation of duties helps keep everyone honest and emphasizes how the board pays close attention to monthly financial statements.

EXCERPT...

Adequacy of Financial Systems and Practices to Manage Federal Funds
[The applicant] follows standard accounting procedures and uses software to track and properly manage federal funds. Each grant is managed as a separate, independent cost center so that expenditures are recorded and reported by grant. Purchases require a purchase order, invoice or receipt in order for funds to be disbursed, and the office staff maintains paper copies of all documentation in secure filing cabinets. Separation of duties between the Executive Director, who draws down federal funds, and the Administrative Assistant, who records bills and presents checks to the Director for signature, help to ensure that funds are handled properly. Any check for $500 or more requires a second signature by a Board Member. Monthly, the entire Board reviews the Statement of Assets and Liabilities, Statement of Last Month's Activity and reviews the check register. This provides total transparency of the organization's finances.

Quality of Personnel

Okay, back to stuff that's a bit more fun. We get to brag again. Don't be fooled by our light tone. Grant reviewers pay close attention to your plan for staffing your grant project and how qualified your proposed personnel are.

Demonstrating Qualifications of Existing Personnel

If your project is led by a principal investigator, such as a research project, or is dependent on your staff being able to successfully follow an existing model, reviewers will pay attention to the qualifications of personnel you already have on staff. They want to know that the person about to lead this project is qualified. You may have to explain your plan to reassign people from their current duties to work on the grant project.

In addition to summarizing your staff's most relevant experience in your narrative, you often attach one or more resumes to the application. Or among academics or medical professionals, the resume may be called a vita, or CV (short for *curriculum vitae*).

Allow time to edit staff resumes if they are required as attachments. People often use quirky fonts in their resumes or may have really small margins that don't meet your RFA's guidelines. You may be limited to only two pages per vita, but they give you fifteen pages listing every article they've ever written. It takes diplomacy and tact to reduce someone else's life down to two pages. Explain that you are allowed only two pages and that you want to keep the focus on the person's skills and experience that are most important to this grant.

practical tip

Demonstrating That Qualified Personnel Will Be Hired

On other occasions, some or all of the grant staff will be new hires. In such instances, you want to provide clear job descriptions for each grant-funded position. These should list the qualifications and experience that you will require.

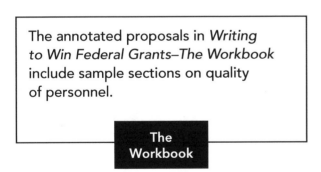

The annotated proposals in *Writing to Win Federal Grants–The Workbook* include sample sections on quality of personnel.

The Workbook

You may also need to explain your hiring procedures or describe how you will advertise for your new staff. If you are located in a rural area or a community that reviewers may perceive to be impoverished, it's a good idea to explain how your organization will be able to attract qualified personnel to its staff.

Be sure to strike a balance in your qualifications between making them so stringent you won't find anyone who meets them and so weak that reviewers are concerned your staff will not be able to handle your project.

Bragging Rights

We admit that most of the content you will write about your organizational capacity will be pretty dry and fact oriented. Brag when you can and when it's accurate. Thank goodness, once this stuff is written, you can use it again and again—usually with only minor updates or tweaks.

To Recap

◆ Organizational capacity is an essential element of your project narrative, even if that title never appears anywhere in the RFA.

◆ Convince reviewers that you have the resources necessary to implement a big, complex project and to sustain it after the grant ends, if necessary.

◆ Assure the funding agency that you have appropriate fiscal controls in place to properly manage its money.

◆ Approach the quality of personnel section strategically. It carries much weight with reviewers.

Chapter Thirteen

Proposal Sections: Evaluation Plan

IN THIS CHAPTER

    ---→ Demystifying evaluation plans

    ---→ Talking about evaluation

    ---→ Working with an external evaluator

    ---→ Other types of evaluation plans

You've designed a great plan to meet an important need in your community. You have described the outcomes you expect to see from your project. Now you get to explain to the funder how you are going to define success and then measure it.

Pull your logic model out and review the goals and objectives you wrote earlier. What did you say you were going to accomplish with this program? Examine your objectives. Can you explain to another person how you will measure them? That's your evaluation plan. Yes, you must be realistic. Perhaps even push a little. But how many times in your life will you get the opportunity to tell someone else the definition of success? Not many.

You're going to have to throw some jargon around to prove you're part of the club, and you might have to create a big, tedious table with lots of detail about measuring and reporting. But, basically, explaining how you will measure each objective is the meat of your evaluation plan.

Demystifying the Evaluation Plan

One way to draft out the outline of an evaluation plan before getting caught up in the details of the RFA's instructions is to think in terms of five important questions. They look deceptively simple, but if you answer them honestly, your answers can help you promise an evaluation strategy you can actually deliver.

When thinking about what should be in your evaluation plan, ask yourself these questions:

1. What do we need to measure (smoking, reading, housing)?

2. When will we need to measure it?

3. How will we measure it? (What tools will be used? Do we already have these tools, or do they need to be developed?)

4. Who will be responsible for doing the measuring and documenting?

5. How will we report it?

A good evaluation plan can be one of the most exciting parts of your proposal. It's where you get to define success. You get to tell the reviewer why settling 10 percent of homeless men into permanent housing and maintaining that housing for twelve months is cause for celebration. Or why having 75 percent of the students you serve reading at grade level within nine months is just short of a miracle.

 practical tip

---

Keep It Real

Cheryl once had a client who set as an objective of its healthy marriages grant to reduce the divorce rate in the service area county by 10 percent in five years. All sorts of red flags went off. First, how would the program staff be able to measure county-wide divorce rates? Then, how could they prove that any reduction could be attributed to their project activities? In reality, grant activities would reach only a few thousand county residents at best. It was a mathematical impossibility for their small project to impact such a large portion of the population. We rewrote the objectives to focus on what the program could measure, such as couples who received services demonstrating improved communication skills on posttests.

 stories from the real world

---

Turn the answers to these questions into an executive summary of your evaluation plan, such as, "1. We will measure student academic progress. 2. We will take these measures every four weeks. 3. To measure student academic success, we will examine grade reports, practice tests, and attendance records. 4. The administrative support technician will collect all of these records and provide them to the project director, who will analyze them. 5. At the end of the academic year, the project director will report on students' progress for the year."

Of course, in an actual evaluation plan, you will have to answer all five questions for more than one objective. But having an executive summary for each objective can help you map out your plan. It can also highlight any potential flaws (such as, do you know the schools will give you student data every four weeks?). Doing a quick overview of your measurement plans can help you promise only what your resources will realistically allow you to do. You may have to go back and edit your original objectives once you realize they will be difficult or expensive to measure the way they were originally written.

One way to keep your evaluation plan manageable is to keep your list of objectives short. We usually recommend focusing on only three to five outcomes if possible. Of course, if you are required to measure predetermined outcomes set by the funding agency, you're stuck having to use them instead, but at least all of your competitors will be in the same boat.

Keeping It Realistic

Probably the most common mistake we see in evaluation plans is promising to accomplish more than is possible. Organizations fall into the trap of overpromising in their evaluation plans in several ways:

1. Asserting that the program can achieve an amount of change disproportionate to the scope of the project (such as promising you can affect 10 percent of the population when your project reaches only 2 percent of the population)

2. Promising to collect more data than is possible with your budget, resources, or expertise (such as promising to administer multiple surveys when your budget has insufficient funds for a person to collect and analyze that much data)

3. Planning to measure something that happens after the grant has ended (such as a three-year program serving high school students that promises to report how many of those students ultimately graduate from college)

4. Designing process objectives instead of outcome objectives (such as planning to measure how many posters you created for your marketing campaign)

If you find yourself creating a list of seven or eight objectives, make sure you are writing outcome objectives and that you aren't falling into the trap of treating your activities as objectives. For example, look at some typical process objectives on the left-hand side of the table below. Every single one of these is covered by the one measurable outcome objective in the right-hand column.

Process Objectives	Outcome Objective
1. Develop a consistent message to promote healthy weight in the target population. 2. Assess current weight status in the target population. 3. Implement a personalized healthy weight plan. 4. Reassess participants' weight annually.	Among adults advised to follow a healthy weight plan, 10 percent will achieve a healthy BMI (body mass index) by the end of three years.

Formative and Summative Evaluation

Now we get to some of those terms we referred to earlier. You will probably talk about formative and summative evaluation quite a bit in your evaluation plans. Administering daily quizzes to make sure students are learning what you are teaching is formative evaluation. Waiting until the end of the semester and giving only a final exam is summative evaluation. Of course, you can, and should, do both.

Formative evaluation is performed during a project, as you are going along. It can focus on the timeline and work plan to make sure you are implementing the activities you said you would. Or it can focus on the recipients of your program. For example, if your objective is that homeless men placed into housing keep that housing for twelve months, you wouldn't wait until the end of the year and just count how many were still housed. You would check in with them regularly to ensure they were not about to lose their housing.

In contrast, summative evaluation is performed at the end of a project (or the end of each project year.) It is used to measure what was accomplished after the fact. Did you serve the number of people you planned to? Did they perform as you predicted (increased test scores, decreased unhealthy behaviors, etc.)?

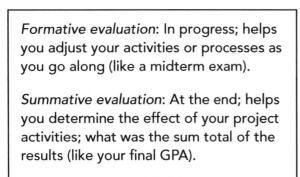

Formative evaluation: In progress; helps you adjust your activities or processes as you go along (like a midterm exam).

Summative evaluation: At the end; helps you determine the effect of your project activities; what was the sum total of the results (like your final GPA).

Postproject summative analysis is essential. It focuses on outcomes, and outcomes are what funding agencies use to prove their programs should continue to receive money from Congress. But RFAs also frequently ask you how you will periodically assess yourself to ensure your project is operating within the budget, adhering to the timeline, and achieving the desired results as you go along.

In the excerpt from an evaluation plan below, we were responding to RFA criteria that asked us to describe how we would undertake "periodic assessment of progress toward objectives and intended outcomes." This is another way of saying "formative evaluation." The program delivered professional development to teachers.

Even though the assessment methods were described in the narrative, we also summarized them into a table that indicated when assessments would take place. The table also proactively links each assessment measure back to the program outcomes.

EXCERPT...			
Periodic Assessment of Progress			
Assessment	What is Measured	When	Related to Outcomes
Staff Meetings	Progress on assignments	Monthly	All
Fiscal Reconciliation	Funds spent in support of activities as planned	Monthly; Annual	All

EXCERPT...

Periodic Assessment of Progress			
Assessment	What is Measured	When	Related to Outcomes
Course Evaluation	Participant perception of quality of courses and teaching	Dec. and May Years 2-5	All, but esp. Obj. 1
Data and Portfolio Review	Course completion, retention, grades, portfolio score	Dec. and May Years 2-5	All, but esp. Obj. 1
Mid-Year Evaluation	Whether tasks are meeting deadlines; enrollment meeting targets	Every April	All
Year-End Evaluation	All data and finances for year; review of all targets	Every September	All

The table below gives you a cheat sheet of formative and summative evaluation methods. Sometimes whether something is a formative measure or a summative measure has more to do with when it is used than what it is. However, this framework can help ensure your evaluation plan contains elements of both.

Formative Evaluation Methods	Summative Evaluation Methods
◆ Monthly reports of usage, attendance, etc. ◆ Pre-/posttests administered for a major activity during the year ◆ Surveys after major activities ◆ Observing services as they are delivered ◆ Progress reports on completion of strategies and any challenges to meeting timeline	◆ Year-end surveys, questionnaires, or tests. ◆ Posttests administered at the end of the project ◆ Reports on year-long participant data, such as attendance at events, results of tests ◆ Annual report to board of directors, funding agency or public

Most of the time, things don't go exactly as planned. When that happens, assess honestly what roadblocks you faced and make a concrete plan to get your project back on track. If it becomes apparent that something will have a significant impact on your budget or ability to meet your objectives, it's usually best to check in with the program officer to propose solutions. Don't surprise the funding agency with bad news at the end of the project period.

Quantitative and Qualitative Data

Now that you've mastered formative and summative evaluation, we turn to data. RFAs will frequently ask you to describe how your evaluation methods will examine both quantitative and qualitative data.

Program Officers Want You to Be Successful

It can be scary to share potentially bad news with your program officer. But it's better to let program officers know in advance if you anticipate difficulty completing an activity or achieving an objective. Sometimes they can even help you develop solutions.

Karen once worked on a project that encountered several challenges, including a strike in a foreign country that threatened the travel plans of an exchange program. She contacted the program officer to explain the situation and propose some options her team had considered. But the program officer offered an alternative Karen didn't even know was possible. Working with the US Embassy, the program officer was able to help the program obtain travel at a reduced rate not available to the public. If the program team members had continued to muddle along on their own, they may not have been able to overcome the travel crisis without a big budget hit or delay in their activities.

stories from the real world

Quantitative data is specific and measurable. Such data elements are often derived from tests, surveys, or other measurements. The results may be compared with a preproject baseline, such as the percentage of students earning grades of "C" or better before receiving tutoring and after tutoring.

Qualitative data is usually less measurable but more descriptive. It can be considered more subjective, but it is just as meaningful and important as quantitative data. You get qualitative data from records like staff logs, meeting notes, or open-ended questions on surveys. Qualitative data may also be obtained by observing services being delivered and taking notes, interviewing individuals, or conducting focus groups. Skilled and trained researchers know how to draw valid conclusions from such sources.

> *Quantitative data*: Numeric measures, obtained from sources such as scores, demographics, or database reports (such as number served, number who improved performance, etc.).
>
> *Qualitative data*: Descriptive or observable data, obtained from sources such as meeting notes, questionnaires, and interviews.
>
> **definition**

The excerpt below was also drawn from the proposal to provide professional development to teachers. This table was prepared in response to the RFA's requirement that applicants "demonstrate they will use both quantitative and qualitative data sources" when evaluating their projects.

EXCERPT...	
Summary of Quantitative Data Elements	
Enrollment Data	• Teacher participant enrollment in each cohort; year-to-year retention

EXCERPT...

Summary of Quantitative Data Elements	
Outcomes Data	• Examples of outcomes data include course success, participant progress, receipt of ESL endorsement, pre & post disposition changes, portfolio assessments, teaching observations
Completion Data	• Teacher completion of the curriculum in each year and at program end
Other Program Data	• Number of courses updated/developed; number of teachers attending ESL symposia; course evaluation results
Summary of Qualitative Data Elements	
Outcomes Data	• Surveys, classroom observations, participant interviews
Program Data	• Course evaluation comments, participant satisfaction/assessment of quality survey, anecdotal responses to ESL symposia

Don't forget. We rarely create a table and drop it into a narrative with no context. Unless we have absolutely no space, we will precede or follow tables like the one in the excerpt above with a narrative description of the most important elements of our plan. The tables are used to support our narrative explanations, not replace them.

Putting It All Together

Almost every funding agency requests something a little different from your evaluation plans. The box below includes an excerpt from one RFA from the Department of Education, with its instructions for what content should be in an evaluation plan. We selected this example because the content written in response includes both formative and summative evaluation and addresses quantitative and qualitative data.

EXCERPT...

(G) Evaluation Plan: The plan should describe the evaluation design, indicating: (1) what types of data will be collected; (2) when data will be collected; (3) what methods will be used; (4) what instruments will be developed and when; (5) how the data will be analyzed; (6) when reports and outcomes will be available. The evaluation plan should indicate what information will indicate if the project is developing in a manner that meets its goals and objectives.

The six items are all important, but imagine trying to explain them in a long narrative description. We had to explain these six points for six required objectives. Are you surprised that we decided it would be easier to communicate our plan in a table?

The excerpt below includes just a few rows of the table we developed in response to that RFA prompt. Because there was so much information required, we had to take extreme measures to fit everything within one-inch margins. All in the name of saving just one more line.

EXCERPT...

Applicant's Quantitative Evaluation Methods				
Dept. Objective	Types of Data Collected	When Collected and Available	Collection Methods & Instruments Used	Analyzed and Used to Improve
Formative evaluative measures are marked with an (F); summative measures with an (S)				
Obj. 1: GPA	- Grade and attendance reports (F) - Transcripts from target high schools (S)	- Every 4.5 weeks and semester - Beginning and end of each semester	Target high schools will document grades on grade reports and GPA on official transcripts	Proj. Dir. and staff analyze to determine eligibility, progress; used to adjust services or change tutoring based on student grades
Obj. 2: Proficient Scores on AIMS Math and Language	- Practice tests (F) - Performance in AIMS prep class (F) - AIMS score (S)	- Annually - Weekly - End of year	Students take practice tests; tutors keep logs of scores; students re-take exam every year until they reach proficient	Dir. & staff analyze; determines need for tutoring/ academic enrichment; used to adjust topics in AIMS workshops to align with greatest need
Qualitative Measures Taken				
All	Interviews	During selection process; when students with-draw or graduate	Entrance interviews of participants and parents); exit interviews of students who leave the program	Director analyzes; assesses need for support services or modify services if needed based on student feedback
1, 2, 3, 4	Tutoring and Advising Logs	Weekly for tutor logs; every 8 weeks for advising logs	Staff and tutors record daily contact and advising logs; entered into database weekly by the Support Tech.	Reviewed by staff; used to intervene if students are missing their obligations and get them back on track

Working with an External Evaluator

So far, we have given examples of evaluation methods that your organization probably has the capacity to perform on its own. However, sometimes you may need to conduct an evaluation that is beyond your own staff's expertise or time. Other times, the funding agency will strongly recommend or require that all grantees use an external evaluator.

Often the external evaluator conducts what is essentially a performance evaluation of the project team in addition to evaluating whether the project reached its objectives. To be considered truly "external," the evaluator must be far enough removed from the project and its staff to be able to give you frank advice.

The amount of work you expect from external evaluators ranges widely. Some merely come in, look over the data you have collected, and make recommendations for improvement or confirm your own analysis. Others remain closely involved in your project from the application stage onward. They may design surveys and other tools and collect or analyze data themselves. If you have a multiple-partner consortium, they may need to collect data from all of your partners and compile it into a coherent whole.

Because of this wide variation in what external evaluators expected to do, their fees can vary dramatically. They usually range from a few thousand dollars per year up to 20 percent of the total grant award, or perhaps even more. See **Appendix J** for tips on how to select an evaluator for your projects.

As odd as it may sound, the "external" evaluator doesn't always have to come from outside your organization. Some organizations such as universities or research organizations have their own assessment departments. As long as this department is separate in the organizational structure from the grant program, then it may be considered an external evaluator. Confirm with the program officer that such an arrangement meets the funder's expectations before assuming it will be acceptable.

Levels of Evaluation

Back in **Chapter Five**, we recommended that you consider the complexity of the expected evaluation when you are making a decision whether to pursue a particular funding opportunity. If you have been following our advice, you probably have at least one outcome objective and maybe two to three process objectives to evaluate. Doing this helps you keep your emphasis on the impact your project activities will have on participants.

Many of you will never be asked to conduct an evaluation beyond that level. However, we do want you to recognize some terms related to more advanced evaluation methods so you will know when it's time to bring in expert help.

One US foundation places evaluation methods into these four categories when it explains grant evaluation to its recipients (Edna McConnell Clark Foundation, emcf.org):

♦ *Completion of program activities.*
Basically counting outputs. We know you know better than to do only this.

♦ *Basic impact on participants.*
Collecting and analyzing basic data that will allow you to draw some conclusions about the impact of your project activities. This is where most of your plans will be.

> *Comparison group*: Group of people chosen for their similarity to the group of people you serve by your project, such as two different third-grade classes (preferably at the same school).
>
>

♦ *Proving impact through comparison groups (quasi-experimental).* Comparing the impact experienced by those you served with what happened in a group of people you did not serve. Can be expensive to implement, so be cautious before promising to use comparison groups.

♦ *Proving impact through randomly assigned control groups (experimental design).* Using a randomized controlled trial to prove that grant activities (and not some other variables) led to the desired impact among program participants. Bring in the experts on something like this.

The table below summarizes the four levels of evaluation and shows how each might be applied to the same grant program. The program will provide financial literacy education to users of a public library. Comparison and control groups could be selected from among library patrons who did not attend the classes.

Snapshot of Evaluation Methods

Evaluation Level	Type of Evaluation	Sample Program Measure
Completion of program activities	Outputs	Two hundred fifty people attend one of ten financial literacy classes
Basic impact on participants	Outcomes	Of those completing the financial literacy curriculum, 75 percent report they will open a savings account.
Proving impact—comparison groups	Quasi experimental (Groups should be as similar as possible but could be just any library patron. Patrons sign themselves up [self-select].)	Of those completing the financial literacy curriculum, 75 percent open a savings account, compared with only 25 percent of those who did not attend.

Snapshot of Evaluation Methods

Evaluation Level	Type of Evaluation	Sample Program Measure
Proving impact—control groups	Experimental (Members of both groups should match demographically. Those who take classes randomly selected from all patrons.)	Of those completing the financial literacy curriculum, 75 percent open a savings account, compared with only 25 percent of those in the control group.

While it may sound like an excellent idea to propose a quasi-experimental design, there can be obstacles to obtaining data on the comparison group. For example, a mentoring program might want to compare the graduation rates of the students it serves with other students attending the same high schools. But this would require them to have access to the data about those other students, and the schools may not release that information. If you cannot access the data you need to evaluate results among comparison groups, you can still have a strong outcomes-based evaluation if you focus on the graduation rates of your students.

Quasi-experimental designs also require potentially complex analysis of data. This can be time consuming and require a certain skill set, so be sure to budget both your time and funds for evaluation accordingly.

Please do not stress about this. Most of you will rarely write a government grant with such complicated evaluation methods. If you do, then your organization probably has internal research resources or you will be working with an outside researcher. Rarely will a grant professional write an experimental evaluation plan without substantial assistance.

To Recap

◆ Strong evaluation plans are absolutely essential to winning the grant.

◆ Most evaluation plans should include both formative and summative strategies and include quantitative and qualitative data.

◆ It's not a plan if you don't know what tools will be used, who will use them, and when they will be used. Include details.

◆ Take your cues from the RFA and the funding agency regarding how complex or simple your evaluation plan is expected to be.

Chapter Fourteen

Until Grant Do Us Part? Partnerships and Collaborations

IN THIS CHAPTER

---> Formalizing informal relationships

---> Creating a Memorandum of Understanding

---> Characteristics of successful partnerships

Working with other organizations is a lot like marriage. Even the best take work. Some partnerships thrive for years without any formal agreements in place. Unfortunately, we've also seen projects and partnerships that fall apart when key staff members change or misunderstandings occur.

Many successful organizations are learning that partnerships help them focus on their core competencies. Budgets no longer support being all things to all people. Funding agencies like the prospect of having greater impact with their grant dollars if they can get all of the similar agencies in a state or region cooperating toward common goals.

Sometimes funding opportunities require collaborations or partnerships. Some even demand that specific types of organizations work together. We've seen collaborations that were as simple as one organization agreeing to provide one service to the grant recipient. We've also worked with consortia of five, ten, or fifteen partners coming together to serve a multistate region or to create international programs.

You probably have natural partners in your community, or you may have already collaborated with other organizations on mutual goals. That's the easiest place to start. Informal partnerships are attractive, because you can move quickly with a minimum of bureaucracy. Other times, you need to formalize the relationship. We'll walk you through the levels of partnerships and how to formalize them when it's time.

Elements of Successful Partnerships

What makes the difference between a good partnership and one that is challenged? In our experience, strong grant partnerships have at least three essential characteristics, regardless of their size or complexity: (1) a desire to work together, (2) a shared vision, and (3) a commitment to sharing.

If you can, look before you leap. Consider whether you and your partners are aligned on these key issues before entering into an agreement that depends on the partnership's success. If you are already collaborating with others, use these elements as a springboard to improve and solidify your relationship:

> What's the difference between a partnership and a collaborative relationship? We would say not much. In common usage, some people consider a partnership to be more formal, maybe even a legal relationship. We really don't care what term you use. Regardless of whether you are collaborating or partnering, our advice will be the same: document, document, document.

1. *Desire to work together and engage in a project.* Can you articulate what it is that all of the organizations involved in the collaboration or consortium want to achieve together? Why is it a good idea to work together, aside from the grant money?

2. *Shared vision.* Are all partners working toward the same outcomes? Can you articulate how working together furthers the mission of each organization?

3. *A commitment to sharing.* Do you need to share any resources to achieve your mutual goals? What information might partners need to share with one another or with the lead applicant? How can partners share data with one another while maintaining confidentiality? If such details are spelled out in writing, that's to everyone's benefit.

> State each partner's role and responsibilities in terms that are as concrete and specific as possible. For example, notice how saying "Organization X and Organization Y will collaborate to serve homeless women," doesn't really tell anyone what is happening. Saying something like "Organization X provides housing and case management to the homeless women served by Organization Y, which provides parenting education" helps everyone understand what their roles are.

The excerpt on the next page shows one way we communicated the roles, responsibilities, and contributions of multiple partners. This document was part of the grant proposal, not a document of agreement among partners. In fact, most agreements to these responsibilities were acquired through email confirmations. The applicant had to execute MOUs only with the schools served in the project.

Space was once again at a premium in the application from which the table below was excerpted, which is why you will see some unavoidable abbreviations.

EXCERPT...				
ROLES OF PROJECT PARTNERS				
Who	What	When	Where	Purpose
Smith County Schools	- transport students to Lead Hill Comm Ctr	- 2 days/week	- From Mt. Peak Elementary	- To transport students safely
	- nutritious snacks for all project students	- every day	- All Centers	- Improve nutrition
	- invite staff and volunteers to trainings	- district staff development	- All Centers	- To train tutors
Clinton Methodist Church	- provide a location for project activities	- 4 days/week	- Serves Polk Elementary	- To provide a safe location for student services
Family Services Network	- provide anti-drug/ anti-violence training - materials for sessions	- entire project	- All Centers	- To deter students from drug use and violence
Adult Basic Ed.	- provide parents with educational classes	- entire project	-Hope High School	-To increase parent success
Montfort College	- provide college students as volunteer tutors	- entire project	- All Centers	- Role models - To tutor students
Chamber of Commerce	- provide business professionals to deliver entrepreneurial training	- quarterly	-All Centers	- To develop entrepreneurship skills

First Steps to Formalizing Relationships

Often organizations develop informal relationships with other nonprofits that can contribute to the success of programs in meaningful ways. A quick phone call or email between staff members who know one another can accomplish a lot.

That personal relationship with an individual at another organization is a strength that enables both organizations to advance their missions. However, failing to make the relationship more formal, so that it's more about the two organizations than the two of you, puts both organizations at risk. You may negatively affect the programs of both organizations programs and the people they serve. We know you don't want that.

Documenting Informal Relationships

Once a collaborative effort grows from a one-time favor into something more long term, it's time to make the relationship more formal. This does not have to be complex or time consuming.

Document, Document, Document—Even If There Are Only Two of You

For more than ten years, a local organization was under contract to a state child welfare organization to provide parenting classes. Since the organization had only a small budget, it depended on volunteers to provide childcare while the parents attended class. The leader of the classes worked informally for several years with one of her friends to provide childcare.

Her friend was the service learning coordinator for a local high school. It was a great program. Students were trained, recruited, and screened as required by the contract. Unfortunately, the partnership was never documented, and there were no volunteer logs.

Then the leader of the parenting program suddenly had to move out of the country with only three weeks' notice when her husband was transferred. No replacement was hired for her until the beginning of the next school year. The program had always operated smoothly in the past, and no one expected any problems. Until they had to figure out how to provide childcare.

Since no one knew or remembered where the childcare volunteers came from, the parenting classes did not start on time, and the organization's contract was in jeopardy. The service learning coordinator from the high school had been seriously ill during this same time. It wasn't until she returned to work and apologized to the organization for not being there to place her students that the organization learned how the childcare had been provided in the past.

We know this kind of sounds like lightning struck twice. The only two people who knew how the relationship worked were both suddenly unavailable at the same time. But obviously it happens! If an MOU had been executed between the two organizations, the program's childcare delivery and parenting classes could have continued uninterrupted no matter what happened to the two key individuals.

 stories from the real world

You can take a big step forward if you document the relationship and what each organization does for the other. Write up a memo explaining the relationship. Send it to people, like your executive director or director of programs, who should be informed. Keep a copy in the files related to that program. Bonus if you send that memo to your partner and your partner responds by email that the memo represents the relationship as the partner understands it. This one simple step can mean the difference between a partnership that thrives and one that is so unstable that the least little change can threaten it.

What information should be included in such a document? You can create or adapt a standard form for your organization to capture key basic information. It should include the following:

◆ Name of the organization with whom you are cooperating

◆ Name of a contact person, with email address and phone number

◆ Name of the program on which you are collaborating

◆ List of what the other organization is contributing (this would be similar to a Scope of Work in an MOU or contract)

> *Writing to Win Federal Grants–The Workbook* provides a "Program Partnership" chart you can use or adapt to collect information about and to document informal relationships that support your organization's programs.
>
> **The Workbook**

◆ Dollar value, if any, of the other organization's contribution to your program (useful, for example, for documenting an in-kind contribution or match)

If you can then get that agreement signed, even better. A signed, formal agreement gives a relationship the best chance of surviving changes in individuals.

> It usually works best for the lead organization or the organization that originally called the partnership together to write the first draft of the MOU. This is especially true if the RFA requires your MOU to include certain information. But expect your partners to have edits or additions. An MOU should establish shared values among partners. Beginning a collaborative agreement by trying to dictate the terms to the other partners is not likely to contribute to a strong, mutually beneficial relationship.
>
>  practical tip

The next step is to evaluate when and how to establish an MOU with partners who are willing to "sign on the dotted line" with you. Generally speaking, you take this step when everyone involved can agree that executing an MOU makes sense—that it lends some type of value to the partners involved and the clients they serve. Of course, sometimes we break out the pens because we have to have a signed MOU to apply for a certain grant.

Building an MOU

MOUs provide evidence of a partnership or collaboration to a federal agency. They should demonstrate the strength of your relationship. Sometimes they are required, and some funding agencies will require specific wording or information. Others won't have this requirement and will accept any format you choose. We strongly recommend you execute an MOU with any partners who are essential to your grant-funded program, even if one doesn't have to be submitted with the proposal. We have seen grants fail and organizations forced to return funds because of partnerships gone south. Think of the MOU like a prenuptial agreement. It spells out how you and your partners will relate, what you will share, what property belongs to each partner, and—should you split—how you will split things.

The content of an MOU varies from agreement to agreement, but most include the following components (we describe the part of the MOU and then include an excerpt from an actual RFA so that you can build one as you go):

◆ Names of the organizations involved

◆ Articulation of a shared vision or purpose

EXCERPT...

"Organization A and Organization B agree that women in their reproductive years are in need of screening, brief intervention, and referral to treatment (SBIRT) services. SBIRT services improve outcomes for both women and their children.

Organization A and Organization B agree that co-locating services at Organization B's facilities is mutually beneficial. Further, Organization A recognizes that its program participants often lack medical homes and experience wait times for health services that interfere with their recovery."

◆ A clear description of what each party is committing to the relationship

EXCERPT...

Organization A will:
1. Serve as the lead organization for purposes of submitting the proposal
2. Manage project activities to ensure objectives are met
3. Coordinate planning and implementation activities and lead project meetings
4. Provide an appropriately credentialed staff member to deliver SBIRT services 8 hours per week at Organization B's facilities
5. Share outcome data with Organization B's staff
6. Maintain confidential records of all patients referred for services

Organization B will:
1. Share information with Organization A for the purposes of grant reporting
2. Provide space for SBIRT services to be delivered on-site at Organization B locations
3. Receive up to six referrals per week from Organization A's participants needing health services
4. Schedule Organization B's staff to participate in SBIRT training

◆ Signatures of all parties

Other items that are often included are the following:

◆ A period of time for the relationship, if relevant

◆ The primary point(s) of contact

◆ How disagreements will be resolved

Please note that MOUs usually do not contain payment terms for services provided. Instead, payment terms and deliverables should be outlined in a separate contract.

You might also include references to other items that are important to your program:

◆ Commitment to shared data and evaluation

◆ Commitment to confidentiality

◆ Communication tools or protocols

◆ Required use of joint or standard resources such as a database

◆ Periodic meetings to assess and review outcomes

MOUs are not rigid documents. They spell out how organizations will work together and support a specific purpose. When written with that expectation in mind, rather than from the mindset of a more rigid contract, they foster the growth and development of a relationship and strengthen your programs.

Collaborations and partnerships grow and evolve. Be prepared to change and adapt as your program or project matures. In fact, include a statement about modifications in any agreements you sign.

Keep your language friendly. Instead of saying "must" or "should" (which imply imperatives), say "intend" or "agree." Use words that establish shared values rather than stiff relationships (i.e., "will work together toward reducing the incidence of premature birth" rather than "are contractually bound to provide services to reduce premature birth"). In most cases, simple versions tend to be the most helpful. Writing in plain language rather than legalese helps too.

Writing to Win Federal Grants–The Workbook includes several sample MOUs/MOAs you can use as models.

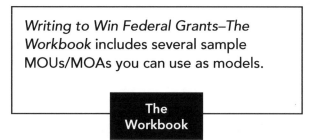

Once you have gathered the basic information about your current partners and collaborators, identify which partnerships are of highest priority to get formalized. Maybe you select those that contribute the most to your program. Or perhaps you decide to start with relationships that you know will be easiest to formalize first to give everyone a taste of success. Success breeds success.

To Recap

◆ Select partners carefully, on the basis of shared vision and values and the potential for mutual benefit.

◆ Informal partnerships run the risk of falling apart when personnel change.

◆ Even if your partnership or collaboration is informal, create a written record of each partner's responsibilities.

◆ An MOU formalizes the relationship among partners or collaborators and sets clear expectations for everyone's participation.

Chapter Fifteen

Submitting Your Application

IN THIS CHAPTER

···→ Finalizing the narrative

···→ Completing standard forms

···→ Adding required attachments

You've spent a lot of time working on the main components of your grant application—the project narrative, budget, and budget narrative. Now we are going to talk about how to finalize those documents so you are ready to submit them.

But wait. There's more! Included with your fifty-page narrative and ten-page budget narrative, you get these five federal forms and ten attachments. Absolutely free.

Well, at least that's how it feels sometimes. You've done all this work. You may be exhausted, and now you have to figure out the difference between an SF-LLL and the Certification Regarding Lobbying. Or maybe there is a required form that wasn't included in the application package, and now you need to track it down.

So we are going to help you sort these out. Some of these items require only a signature from someone like your executive director. You can do that as soon as the RFP comes out. And you probably already have some of the most commonly requested attachments handy. Like so many other things about federal grants, if you can read a checklist and follow every single detail, you can handle this.

Finalizing Your Narrative

Once you've written the entire narrative, if you have time, set it aside for a day or two while you work on forms or some other part of the application. Try to finish up writing early enough that you can give the document to a colleague to review for you. Find one of those super detail-oriented people and turn them loose on your narrative.

We know, it can be a little scary to hand over this baby you've nurtured from its beginnings, but thoughtful comments from a good reader will strengthen your proposal. Ask the person to pretend to be a grant reviewer. Provide the RFA or a mock score sheet. Emphasize that you are looking for an assessment of clarity, organization, and responsiveness to the RFA. Otherwise, people will tend to focus on proofreading or personal style rather than substantive issues.

Most of the time, you will convert your documents to PDF before submitting them. The software to do this has improved over the years, but both Karen and Cheryl have experienced PDF glitches.

One of Karen's documents once had an extra page created when it was converted from Word to PDF. No one realized this, and the application was eliminated from consideration because it exceeded the page limit. Cheryl once realized that her converted PDF documents had been slightly "shrunk." The giveaway was the larger margins, but those were created because the text was no longer really twelve-point font.

It's also good to have someone who can proofread for you. You do want to submit a proposal that has "excellence" stamped all over it. There is a very real sense among reviewers that if you cannot be careful and accurate in your writing, you might not be careful and accurate in managing federal funds. But here is a little secret—a typo won't kill your proposal. Missing a single point can.

While you are waiting for final comments to come back on your narrative, here are some tasks you can be working on to polish the narrative for submission:

◆ *Create a table of contents.* Check your RFA. This may be required. Sometimes it counts against your page limits, but other times it doesn't. If it isn't required, some of us include them anyway, and others choose not to.

◆ *Double-check page numbers.* We print out the document or scroll page by page to make sure each page is correctly numbered. Sometimes strange word processing codes or a section break can restart page numbering.

◆ *Put in headers or footers.* Check the RFA for any instructions. Even if there are none, we recommend putting your organization's name in the header or footer if allowed.

◆ *Tweak page breaks.* Once we know all corrections are entered, we scroll through the document looking for widows and orphans or tables that break in inconvenient places. Whenever we can, we adjust text so that page breaks don't come in confusing places.

◆ *Check file names.* Many RFAs have precise rules about how your files should be named or rules about no more than a certain number of characters, no spaces, or no symbols. They mean it.

◆ *Double-check formatting requirements.* Sometimes your editor or proofreader may change the font or margins, and sometimes pasting in text provided by someone else does not match the formatting.

◆ *Manually check your budget numbers.* Get out your calculator and add up all your budget numbers, horizontally and vertically. Make sure that those five hundred binders you said would each cost $5 are coming out to be $2,500 in your totals column. While spreadsheets are very handy in creating the budget, it is easy to make a mistake in a formula, such as to miss a few cells or for totals to be $1 off (usually because of rounding).

After the final edits and all of your double-checking details, it's time to finalize your narrative. If you are uploading files into an online submission system, watch that your files don't exceed any maximum file size limits. If you anticipate you may have any difficulties with submitting online, read the RFA carefully for its instructions on how to request a waiver from online submission or alternate submission formats allowed.

Believe it or not, some state agencies that are distributing federal funds require applicants to mail in paper copies of their applications. Other federal agencies require you to record a tracking number after you have submitted, or to send a signed form by fax or paper mail. We've said it so many times that you can probably repeat our advice in your head now: Just pay attention to the RFA's instructions. Never assume anything.

"Standard" Federal Forms

Federal grant proposals share many elements. Most have a cover page that identifies the applicant and provides some basic information about the proposed project. They usually have a specifically required budget form. There are also documents called "certifications and assurances" that indicate the grantee (your organization) will do certain things if you get the grant.

The forms you need for your proposal are not always inside the application package you downloaded. If they are not, use the RFA to make a list of every form you need to complete. If a required form is missing from your application package, you can obtain one online. Start with your funding agency to see if it provides links to forms. Grants.gov also maintains a collection of most of the forms a federal agency would require you to submit.

> Karen once sent a collection of proposal documents to her client, ready for the client to submit. For some reason, a person at the client organization decided it would be a good idea to rename all of the files and change the font. Fortunately, they sent the documents back to Karen for a final check before submitting, and she was able to catch this mistake before the proposal was submitted. Otherwise, it probably would have been rejected for not complying with the RFA requirements.

 stories from the real world

Whether the forms are provided in your downloaded application package or you have to go find them, it's a good idea to make sure you review and know how to fill out each form early on in the application process—don't leave them for the last week. Remember that the closer you get to the deadline, the more rushed (and prone to errors) you will be. Knowing what forms you need, making a list, and completing and gathering them early will save you stress later.

In most instances, the guidelines will either provide actual instructions for completing each of the forms or refer you elsewhere for directions.

SF, such as SF 424, stands for "Standard Form." Unfortunately, not every federal agency uses the same version of the "standard form," and some don't even use the standard forms. Just be sure you read the instructions in the guidelines to be sure you fill out the forms that are required.

Commonly Used Forms

Here is a list of the most commonly requested forms, accompanied by a brief description that points out important details to notice about the form.

SF-424

Titled the "Application for Federal Assistance," the SF-424 is also sometimes called the "cover sheet." This form summarizes data about the applicant, the project, and the budget. You enter your organization's contact information, tax identification number, DUNS number, the project start and end dates, and the congressional districts served. When you press the "submit" button, you will provide the signature of the person authorized to sign your grant proposal. This person is known as the authorized organizational representative, or AOR.

SF-424A

Titled "Budget Information – Non-Construction Programs," the SF-424A is where you enter your proposed budget. Be aware that the funding agency to which you are applying may wish you to use a modified 424A or may have an agency-specific budget form.

On the budget form, you enter the totals in each budget category. If you are applying for a multiyear program, some agencies require you to enter your budget for every year. Others tell you explicitly to include only the budget for year one. The numbers entered into this form need to match the numbers in your budget narrative. It sounds simple, but mistakes do happen when working across documents. Actually, the budget form is a good double-check of your budget narrative. We often find little mistakes in our budget that everyone missed until we started putting numbers into the SF-424A.

SF-424B (Assurances – Non-Construction Programs) or SF-424D (Assurances – Construction Programs)

The assurances documents "certify" or "assure" the federal government that you are in compliance with the statements contained in the assurances. Because the assurances commit your organization to following federal regulations, you need an attorney or your executive director to review them carefully before signing the document. Here's the good news: The assurances document rarely changes. If you know you are going to be applying for a federal grant, go get one of these now and get it approved when it's not urgent.

Insist that someone in senior leadership sign this document. Keep a copy in your file, even if you submit all grants electronically.

SF-LLL

The SF-LLL is a form regarding lobbying. If you are a nonprofit, you likely do not have a lobbyist. However, you still need to fill out the form with the applicant organization's name and then indicate "not applicable" in the first and last name boxes on the form in the sections titled "Name and Address of Lobbying Registrant" and "Individual Performing Services."

Faith-Based EEO Survey

This form collects basic data about organizations applying for federal grants. It's usually optional, but it helps the government keep track of how many faith-based organizations receive grants and how small or large they are. Since the form asks for information about the size of your staff and budget, we recommend updating it once per year.

If you are applying through Grants.gov, there is a section titled "Mandatory Documents" on the "Grant Application Page." Don't assume that this contains every "mandatory document." Always compare the mandatory documents listed in the guidelines with those in the list. Also, do not assume that documents in the "Optional Documents" list are actually optional. Something required may be there instead. Then again, you may have to go searching for a form that was omitted from the package.

Project/Performance Site Location(s)

This form is pretty clear. The funding agency wants you to say where your project or program will take place. If you will have multiple locations, provide the address of each site.

Miscellaneous Other Forms

Other agencies will have forms that you may need to complete. For example, the Department of Education may require a form called "Certification Regarding Debarment, Suspension, Ineligibility and Voluntary Exclusion." The Department of Health and Human Services requires you to submit a form that you are a drug-free workplace.

This is important enough to repeat. Print out the assurances (the SF-424B), and have your executive director (or whomever signs contracts) sign a hard copy. Keep a copy in your files. This way you are off the hook if the person who signed the assurances failed to read and understand them!

Attachments

Some programs may require you to submit as many as twenty different attachments to your application, while others allow you to submit almost no attachments. Since every funding agency has different requirements, just do what the RFA says for the particular opportunity for which you are applying.

> *Writing to Win Federal Grants–The Workbook* includes actual copies of all of these forms, along with notes about how to complete them accurately. These are only examples, however. Any federal agency can change how it wants a form completed at any time. You are ultimately responsible for following the instructions for your particular application.
>
>

Sometimes the RFA will require you to place a header on all your attachments. Even if this is not required, it is a good idea to place your organization's name and DUNS number in a header or footer. If there is room, include the name of the document too.

These can look like this:

◆ Header—Doing Good Services Organization, Pennsylvania DUNS #555000555

◆ Footer—Attachment 3: Organizational Chart Page 1 of 1

When assembling your attachments, do not add any extras beyond those that are requested. On the other hand, if an attachment is required that is not relevant to you, it's safer to include an attachment that says, "This attachment is not applicable to ABC Organization."

Also pay attention to page limits. Anything you do that seems to not follow the instructions means the funder may not have to review your proposal. Sometimes the RFA is so convoluted regarding which attachments and forms will count against your page limits and which are freebies that we have put together a spreadsheet to keep track of this.

With that in mind, here are some of the most commonly requested attachments:

◆ *501(c)(3) letter from the Internal Revenue Service (IRS).* This is used to prove that you meet the eligibility guidelines when applications are restricted to nonprofit organizations.

◆ *Key staff resumes.* Some agencies (such as the National Institutes of Health) will have a required two-

> *Writing to Win Federal Grants–The Workbook* includes a sample spreadsheet that we use to track page limits when that gets a little complicated. We call it a "page budget." One of the annotated proposals in the workbook includes the attachments that were submitted with it so that you can see these recommendations about labeling attachments being enacted.
>
> **The Workbook**

page format. Others may just place a page limit on resumes. Sometimes you can substitute a biosketch for a resume.

◆ *Job descriptions.* Often you need to provide job descriptions for grant-funded positions you will fill only after you receive the grant. Other times, we have been asked to include job descriptions of existing staff positions.

◆ *Organizational charts.* You may be asked to submit an organizational chart for your entire organization, one that's just for the project, or both. If you are applying as part of a consortium or other partnership, you will probably be requested to insert a chart that makes the lines of communication and authority clear in such relationships. We find that we often have to reformat organizational charts so they meet guidelines for margins and font size or need to simplify overcomplicated ones. We also usually take out people's names and replace them with positions or titles.

Your proposal can be kicked out if you don't include an attachment, even if that attachment is not relevant to you! A colleague of ours once was responding to an RFA that required an attachment describing any prior funding the applicant had received from the agency. Since this organization had never received a grant from that funder, he thought he was safe not including that attachment. Wouldn't you?

Unfortunately, the funding agency declared his application nonresponsive and did not score it. Not even appealing to the applicant's senator was enough to overcome this bureaucratic nightmare. Lesson learned, but boy, was it a painful one.

The next application to this funding agency included an attachment that was largely blank except for this sentence: "The ABC organization has received no prior funding from the XYZ agency."

Writing to Win Federal Grants— The Workbook includes several organizational charts in different formats. Annotated proposals include their personnel plans and job descriptions when relevant. The workbook also provides more guidance on writing and obtaining letters of support, including some sample letters.

The Workbook

◆ *Letters of support.* Letters of support are like references. Other organizations or community or political leaders offer their recommendation to the federal agency, essentially testifying as to why your organization is the best to implement a project. Make sure these letters are specific to your project rather than a general letter of endorsement.

◆ *Citations.* In some applications, casual in-line references or footnotes are all that are required. Definitely don't use

We recommend that you offer draft content for people who are signing letters of support for you. This is one way you can ensure the letter meets the requirements of the guidelines. Do be careful to write different versions for all of your supporters to use. Reviewers definitely notice letters of support that all say the same thing.

up one of your precious pages to attach a list of citations if it is not required. But they are sometimes required, such as for the National Science Foundation. In those cases, format your references as required by the RFA. If the guidance says to attach a list of citations, don't title your attachment "bibliography."

◆ *Logic model.* Usually, you can create a logic model in a Word document. Some agencies, such as Housing and Urban Development (HUD), have you create a logic model by making selections from a drop-down menu. If the RFA does not tell you how to format your logic model, use your own format.

◆ *Evaluation tools.* Some agencies will ask you to provide citations of the evaluative tools you intend to use. Others will ask for actual copies of any surveys or other data collection instruments you plan to use.

We have discussed several of the most common items you will be required to attach to your grant proposals. The list of other things that you might be required to include is a bit long. It could include such items as drawings or plans related to construction or renovation activities, results of previous evaluations of your services, your articles of incorporation, a roster of all program partners in the case of a consortium or partnership proposal, a letter of agreement from your external evaluator, and so on.

Finally, we want to provide an additional word of caution about attachments. An RFA to which we were responding recently provided an extensive list of every required attachment, from Attachment 1 to Attachment 15. The problem was, this list conflicted with other information in the guidelines about which attachment should be numbered what. In such a situation, you must ask the program officer to tell you which instruction is correct.

While it is tempting to leave the attachments for the last thing (thinking they're easy), please don't! As soon as you decide to pursue an RFA, start working on any attachments that require information or content from other people or organizations.

Some deadlines list a time by which the application must be received by Grants.gov as well as a date. It may sound silly, but don't forget the difference in time zones. A grant that is due by 4:30 p.m. Eastern time on the deadline date must be submitted by 1:30 p.m. Pacific time and even earlier for applicants in Alaska or Hawaii.

Hitting the Submit Button

If you're like us, sitting in front of your screen once everything is done, facing that "submit" button can bring on a little anxiety. No matter how well prepared you are, no matter how carefully you have checked every detail, hitting "submit" feels so final.

We know it seems impossible, but try your best to submit two to three business days before the actual deadline. This lesson was driven home to us again this year. We know of one applicant to a federal program who hit the "submit" button just thirty minutes before the deadline and then had to watch in dread as the cursor just circled and circled and the clock ticked down. Finally, at the last minute, the application went through. What a nail-biter!

If you submit your proposal early, that gives you some cushion against technical problems on the funder's side or mistakes on your side.

Submit Early

Most of the time, you are allowed to resubmit an application if your first submission had an error or was missing something. But you can resubmit only up until the deadline. After the deadline, no updates may be submitted.

Grants.gov promises to notify applicants within forty-eight hours if their applications have technical errors. If you submit three days before the deadline and you get one of those Grants.gov notices, you have a day to make your corrections and resubmit. If you submitted on the day of the deadline and then get a Grants.gov notice, you are out of luck.

practical tip

After Submitting

Okay, you've worked up the nerve and finally hit "submit." It's gone. You're done. (Except for those few odd agencies that still want you to send in a paper form after the fact, and the National Endowment for the Arts, which asks for samples of artists' work to be sent in the next few weeks.)

Ahhhh, blissful peace. In fact, it may get too peaceful. You will probably wait for months before hearing any news at all about your application. So give yourself a moment to recover and refuel so you are ready to get back to work. But sleep in just one morning or next weekend if you can. Take a long lunch to celebrate. A massage or mindless movie would be good.

You have accomplished something incredible for your organization—something you may have even feared you could not do. But we knew you could do it. You can learn this. Now that you've gotten started, go check out **Appendix L** for additional resources to help you continue developing your federal grant-seeking skills.

To Recap

◆ Don't get so caught up in working on your narrative that you forget to work on your attachments.

◆ Most of the forms you attach to federal applications are relatively standard, and once you've completed them once, you won't have to learn how to do it again.

◆ Spend some time polishing your narrative and your attachments so they are all labeled clearly and conform to the requirements for margins, font size, file names, and any other strange rules the funder throws at you.

◆ Always submit early. Much heartache and stress can be avoided by getting your proposal in early.

Chapter Sixteen

After the Award: Grants Management Tips

IN THIS CHAPTER

- ┄→ The grant professional's role in grants management

- ┄→ What to do after the award

- ┄→ Communicating with program officers

- ┄→ When things go wrong

Congratulations! You just won a federal grant. You have our deepest condolences. One of the best-kept secrets of the grants profession is that writing the grant is the easy part. Implementing the grant may give you heartburn.

You may have thought your job was over once you hit "submit." Not so. You will probably play some role in managing the grant after it is awarded, and that's the way it should be.

Even if your organization is large enough to maintain a postaward office, you need strong relationships with the postaward personnel. You will also be more successful if you have a basic understanding of the principles of postaward management and reporting.

The Grant Professional's Role in Grants Management

In some organizations, the person who prepares grant proposals may wear multiple hats. In fact, we know some of you are program or finance staff, and you are just squeezing grant-writing duties in among everything else. However, as the person at your organization most knowledgeable about what you promised to do (in the proposal) and what the agency expects you to do (in the RFA), we have found that the preaward people (that's you) need to keep their fingers in the postaward pie. Here are some of the reasons why:

Just as stewardship of your individual donors is an essential part of the donor cycle, good grants management is a cultivation strategy. When our bosses used to ask us why we were wasting time going to meetings with the project director to determine how grant funds were being used instead of writing another proposal, we always reminded them of this concept: If our organization develops a bad reputation as a grant recipient, it will damage our chances of winning future grants.

important

◆ How you manage a grant impacts future fundability. A multiyear grant award usually requires an annual report summarizing your progress toward meeting project objectives and on budget expenditures before the funds for the next program year are released to you.

◆ The grant professional is often the one who must write and/or submit reports. Believe us, you don't want to find out that activities are not taking place or funds are not being spent as planned on the day the report is due!

◆ As the proposal writer, you are likely in the best position to advise other staff members about the requirements of the grant, what expenditures are allowable, and what deliverables were promised.

◆ As the proposal writer, you may be aware of certain odd requirements from the funding announcement, such as the Fly America Act (which requires an organization with grant-funded international travel to have personnel fly as far as they can to their destination on an American-flagged airline). With that knowledge, you can help your organization avoid making bad mistakes.

Monitoring the Grant as You Go Avoids Unpleasant Surprises

Reporting is important. Filing accurate reports, on time, is critical. Making sure they reflect that you're doing what you said you would do is imperative. Not everyone understands this.

Once Karen found many errors in the financial information that was to accompany her narrative report on a grant in progress. Unfortunately, the financial report included miscategorized expenses, unallowable expenses, and inadequate matching funds. No wonder the finance staff had been complaining about the grant. They didn't understand it.

Had the report been submitted without Karen's review, the organization would have been in serious trouble with its program officer. But since she was involved, she was able to correct the financial information and help avert future bookkeeping errors. Unfortunately, we have both had too many similar experiences. The preaward staff must always remain vigilant about reporting and spending postaward.

stories from
the real world

What to Do after the Award

There is nothing quite as exciting (at least professionally) as opening a letter that congratulates your organization on an award of $675,000. We know we still celebrate every time we win a grant. But after that dust settles, what's next?

We recommend that you develop some standard postaward procedures. These can help ensure a smooth handoff to the postaward office, if you are fortunate enough to have one. Otherwise, following these steps will help make your postaward life less stressful. It is wise to check up on all these steps:

◆ *Notifying.* Who needs to know you won the award? Internally, your boss, the executive director, program staff, finance staff, and the board of directors. Externally, you will want to share the news with your partners and maybe issue a press release.

◆ *Reading the grant award.* Even though you probably are not the person who signs the grant agreement, you should read it carefully. Make sure you understand your budget, deliverables, and reporting requirements. Then make sure the contract is signed by the proper person and returned to the funder promptly. Keep a copy in your office.

> Sometimes a grant is awarded for less than you requested. Usually, this requires you to do a postaward budget modification. Talking with your program officer can help determine what you should cut from the budget and if you are allowed to cut your expected deliverables by a proportional amount. Sometimes the program officer won't allow you to reduce your outcomes even if the agency has reduced your budget.
>
> Karen once had a grant that was funded at less than half what was requested. A change that drastic would have gutted the project. In that situation, the organization reluctantly decided it had to decline the grant funding.
>
> practical tip

◆ *Thanking.* Funded or not, it's a nice touch to send a thank-you to the program officer. You may also want to consider thanking your legislators if they had a hand in supporting your application. Finally, thank the individuals/organizations that wrote letters of support.

◆ *Award processing.* While you rarely have to do the bookkeeping yourself, if federal grants are new to your organization, you may have to explain the federal way of doing things to your accounting staff. Work out with them a system to track your grant funds separately and to align your chart of accounts with your budget's line items. Give them a copy of the grant budget and budget narrative and enlist their help in heading off any inappropriate expenditures.

Writing to Win Federal Grants–The Workbook includes a form you can use to provide a one-page summary of each grant you have been awarded. This helps your organization keep track of what resources it has promised as part of a match and if it has to raise matching funds. It also contains a sample postaward form you can use to ensure you notify everyone in your organization who should be notified about the grant award.

The Workbook

◆ *Holding a postaward meeting.* Get into the habit of holding a postaward meeting. Of course, you can celebrate. But you also need to convene and educate the project director(s), accounting staff, human resources staff, and any others who will play a role in managing or evaluating the project. At this meeting, review the budget (what costs are allowable), federal regulations related to the project, and reporting deadlines. Decide on a schedule to monitor grant activities, the budget, and reporting.

Right after the grant is awarded is the time to clearly identify roles, responsibilities, and deadlines. Don't assume. Write them down and circulate them after the meeting. And ensure that every required task has a specific person assigned to it. Put dates and deadlines into a central calendar and your calendar.

◆ *Establishing management procedures.* Whenever you receive a new grant award, it is a good time to review your grants management procedures and decide if any need updating or added. Sometimes you may need to adapt to meet the requirements of a particular program. For example, different agencies have different rules about when you have to request permission to make budget changes and what you can change without requesting prior approval.

Getting Budget Changes Approved Postaward

It happens all the time. The price of an item suddenly jumps between the time a proposal is submitted and when the expenditure must be made. We've had it happen to everything from twenty-dollar workbooks to the structural steel needed to complete a capital project.

For something as small as the workbooks, the solution was to find another item in the budget that could be underspent (in this case, travel was going to cost less than planned). Knowing that the regulations in this specific instance allowed grantees to move up to $2,500 between budget line items allowed the grant recipient to solve the problem without having to seek permission from the program officer. Being able to show this rule to the organization's finance director and auditors satisfied their concerns about making a change. The books were ordered and delivered. Project saved.

Other times the solution won't be as simple, and you will have to get permission from your program officer to adjust your budget.

stories from the real world

◆ *Implementing project activities.* Rarely is the grant professional expected to deliver project activities, but we have seen it happen. Your proper role is to answer any questions the project personnel may have and to receive regular reports of grant activities so you can ensure compliance with the approved work plan.

◆ *Reporting and stewardship.* Know your reporting requirements. You often need information from your organization's database or financial records, and this can take time to gather. If others are responsible for creating the report, you need to review it to make sure activities are happening as promised in the original application. You often begin working on your report weeks in advance of the deadline.

> Whenever you make any changes to your planned activities or to the budget postaward, document the changes with a memo to the file. In the memo, explain why you needed to make the change and how your new plans still align with the funding agency's requirements. Having this documentation on hand can save the day if you are audited.
>
>

Communicating with Program Officers

Contact your program officer to introduce yourself. Always ask about program officers' preferred communications styles and if they want additional information from you beyond the required reports. Sometimes they do, and sometimes they don't. It's always nice to be able to give them a quick anecdote if they need one for a report or presentation to a congressional committee.

Please remember that federal program officers want you to be successful and are intended to be an asset to you. If you are successful with your program/project, then they are successful and will share that information with Congress to justify continuance of the program and its funding.

No-Cost Extensions

Sometimes, despite your best management practices and best planning, things still do not go as planned. You crafted a precise timeline, only to find out that the date you intend to begin delivering services is impossible due to hiring delays.

> *No-cost extension:* Allowing a grant recipient more time to reach project outcomes without awarding any additional grant funds.
>
> definition

Other events may conspire to delay the date you can begin delivering services by several months. Or, perhaps, not enough people participated in your program to expend all of the budgeted funds within the grant year.

If you are getting close to the end of a grant year and find that you have significant funds not expended, you can sometimes request a no-cost extension. A no-cost extension allows you to extend your original timeline and continue to expend grant funds from the current year.

No-cost extensions are harder to get than they used to be. That's why it is important to talk with your program officer about any project delays early in the year and not wait until the last minute.

When Things Go Wrong

Maybe a partner who was responsible for essential services suddenly leaves your project. Maybe a key staff member quits. Maybe your referrals suddenly dry up due to a policy change. Let's face it; things sometimes go wrong. Sometimes these things are within your control, and sometimes they're not. What do you do?

When you encounter a problem that is larger than you can solve yourself or that threatens the program's ability to deliver required outcomes, don't hesitate to reach out to your program officer. Hiding things never makes them any easier. Waiting to tell your program officer delays the pain and punishment, but at what cost?

Making the Best of a Worst-Case Scenario

A federal audit is no fun. Especially if the program staff have been lax about record keeping. Karen was hired by an organization in the fourth year of a five-year grant to help prepare for a forthcoming audit.

The files were a mess, and so was the program. Documentation was missing. Some expenditures did not follow the proper bidding process. Documentation of volunteer time, which was part of the required match, was partially missing. Some participant records did not follow the program's requirements.

So Karen called for a thorough internal audit before the external auditors arrived. The internal audit allowed the organization to show the auditors what had happened to the program up to that point and was honest about what could be documented and what could not. The work put into that internal audit showed the auditors that the organization was serious about correcting its past mistakes.

Being forthcoming made all the difference. Instead of losing its grant or having to return the funds for an entire year, the organization had to repay only a minimal amount of grant funds. The truly amazing thing was that the organization received its fifth year of funding. And once it proved that the program was being well managed, the organization received funds for an additional three years. The internal audit had saved the day.

stories from
the real world

However, do your best to be solution oriented. Don't just bring news about a problem. Explain and document what went wrong. Review all your documents, and emphasize any successes you achieved before the project got derailed.

A final word of advice. Documentation is king. We save copies of emails to and from program officers, especially as they relate to changes in our program or budget. Document how you selected vendors and consultants. If bids were required, keep copies of the requests for bids as well as the bids themselves. Similarly, file documentation of all expenditures. Document everything you can. You will be glad you did. Never rely on your memory.

All of the advice given in this chapter is designed to help make your job easier. The time spent in educating your colleagues about how grants work will help avoid mistakes in implementing the project. Working with program staff to make sure you are collecting the right information about the people they serve makes writing year-end reports much smoother.

Face it. You wouldn't have to do post award management if you had not turned in an awesome grant application that got funded. We knew you could do it.

To Recap

◆ Effective grants management helps ensure that your project operates smoothly, problems are addressed effectively, and there are no surprises for the program officer.

◆ The grant professional must stay apprised of how the grant activities are progressing and grant funds are being expended to avoid unpleasant surprises.

◆ Program officers will be your advocate whenever possible, but make their jobs easier by proposing solutions when you explain about problems.

Appendix A

Glossary

A-133 audit: A standard set of financial audit requirements based on OMB Circular A-133. Any organization receiving $750,000 or more in federal funds annually (as of December 2014) must complete an A-133 audit using external auditors.

Action plan: A name for a table, chart, or narrative description of major grant activities, usually including who is responsible for implementing activities and when the activities will take place. Interchangeable with *work plan.*

Administrative overhead: A common term for indirect costs, the administrative costs to an organization of implementing a grant-funded project that cannot be tied specifically and directly to an individual grant program.

Agency: General term used to describe the federal office or department that makes grant awards. HUD, or Housing and Urban Development, is an agency.

Allowable costs: Items that the funding agency says grant funds may be expended on, such as personnel, travel, and supplies.

Assurances: A document an applicant signs or a statement included in an application that "assures" the funding agency that the applicant complies with particular regulations or agrees to follow the funding agency's processes.

Baseline: A number that indicates the rate at which something is happening now, before you deliver your program services.

Baseline data: A data measure of an existing circumstance against which progress made by grant activities is measured.

Benchmark: A criterion by which the performance or success of a grant project is measured, usually a comparison with a fixed target.

Budget: Detailed plan for how grant funds will be spent.

Budget narrative: A written explanation of planned budget expenses, including how cost estimates were developed.

Catalog of Federal Domestic Assistance (CFDA): A collection of all federal funding programs in one listing.

Certifications and assurances: Standard forms that are attached to most federal applications that require the applicant to certify that it adheres to certain federal policies and regulations and to assure that it will remain in compliance during the grant period.

CFDA number: A number issued to each grant opportunity by the Catalog of Federal Domestic Assistance. CFDA numbers usually stay the same from a program's inception onward. The numbers usually take the format of xx.xxx.

Circular: A document published by the Office of Management and Budget (OMB).

Comparison group: A group of people chosen for their similarity to the group of people you serve by your project, such as two different third-grade classes (preferably at the same school).

Competitive preference priorities: An agency may decide that it will award extra points to applications having a certain focus, reaching a certain population, or delivering a particular service.

Consortium: A collection of two or more partners who enter into a written agreement to cooperate on the delivery of services or implementation of a grant project.

Cooperative agreement: Differs from a grant award in that it involves "substantial involvement" of the federal agency in carrying out or evaluating grant activities.

Cost principles: These spell out the government's rules regarding what funds may and may not be spent on. They now appear in Title 2 of the Code of Federal Regulations (CFR).

Cost-reimbursement basis: Being able to draw down/receive funds only when allowable costs have been incurred. Typically, documentation proving funds expenditures must be provided.

Curriculum vitae, or CV: The resumes of professional staff. In singular form, sometimes abbreviated as *vita*.

Direct costs: Things bought and paid for by the grant funds that can be clearly attributed to grant activities, such as paying a driver to transport children to a grant-funded activity.

Draw down: The method by which most grant recipients receive their federal grant funds—logging onto a payment system and submitting an electronic request that the grant funds be transferred into the grant recipient's bank account.

Encumber: Setting funds aside for a specific expenditure in the future.

Evaluation plan: A narrative description of what steps will be taken when, by whom, and by what methods to evaluate the success of the grant-funded project in reaching project outcomes.

Evidence based: A concept or program design that replicates or is similar to a program that has documented evidence of success, usually in the form of studies or published journal articles.

Experimental design: Evaluating the effects of your grant-funded intervention by comparing the results among those served by the grant with a randomly assigned control group; usually requires an experienced researcher to implement properly.

External evaluator: An individual or firm contracted to assess the compliance, performance, and success of the grant-funded project. Generally an objective third-party not directly associated with the grant.

Federal Register: A daily publication that consolidates announcements regarding rules, public notices, and requests for proposals from all federal agencies.

Formative evaluation: Assessing the progress and success of program activities as the program is going on for the purpose of quickly making changes during the project period if planned objectives are not being reached.

Freedom of Information Act (FOIA): A law that gives you the right to access information from the federal government.

Funding opportunity number: A number issued by the funding agency to identify a grant announcement, such as HRSA-12-157.

Generally Accepted Accounting Principles (GAAP): Demonstrating that the applicant organization follows good accounting practices.

Goal: A statement of a desired big-picture outcome or long-term effect on the community or world.

Grant period: The length of time for which an award is made. Project starting and ending dates can usually be found on one's *Notice of Grant Award*.

Grants.gov: An online system to search for and apply for grants from the federal government. Requires free registration.

Guidance/guidelines: The rules agencies publish about the content and format of your proposal. Also called the *RFA* or *NOFA*.

Indirect costs: The expenses an organization incurs to implement a grant-funded project that are not directly attributable to grant activities. Also called *facilities and administrative costs*, or *F&A*.

In-kind contributions: Resources, including portions of a person's time, that are provided by the applicant or by other donors toward the success of the grant project.

Inputs: A term related to building logic models, referring to the resources needed to be "put into" a project or effort in order for that effort to succeed.

Intermediary organization: A grant recipient that has authority to re-award or subaward grant funds to other recipients following prescribed guidelines.

Intervention: A common way to refer to services delivered to a population, e.g., tutoring delivered to third graders is the "intervention."

KSAs: A commonly used acronym for knowledge, skills, and abilities.

Logframe: Short for "Logical Framework Approach." A term more commonly used in international organizations for a chart or graph that is the same as a logic model.

Logic model: A table or chart that summarizes the critical elements of a project, such as inputs, activities, outputs, outcomes, and impact.

Matching funds: Dollars provided by the applicant or its partners to match the amount provided by the federal agreement, based on a ratio set by the funding agency, such as one to one.

Mission creep: The tendency for a task or project to stretch beyond an organization's actual mission without a strategic decision enabling the growth.

Memorandum of Understanding (MOU): A formal written agreement among partners in a grant-funded program that spells out each partner's roles, responsibilities, and commitments. Also called a *Memorandum of Agreement (MOA)*.

Need: The problem or shortcoming in the community that the applicant plans to address with grant funds. Usually required to be documented by recent data but may be supported by anecdotal evidence as well.

No-cost extension: An agreement possibly granted by the funding agency that allows the grant recipient organization to complete project activities beyond the original end of the project year or grant period.

Notice of Grant Award (NGA): A letter or form received from a funding agency notifying an applicant that a grant, contract, or loan has been awarded.

Notice of Funding Availability (NOFA): See *guidance/guidelines*.

Objective: A specific and measurable result of an activity or project that contributes to reaching a larger, long-term goal.

Office of Management and Budget (OMB): Used to produce publications, called circulars, that grant applicants needed to consult. Most OMB circulars have now been combined into the *Uniform Administrative Requirements, Cost Principles, and Audit Requirements for Federal Awards*, accessed at federalregister.gov.

Organizational capacity: The resources, space, expertise, and personnel that an applicant has that indicate it will be successful in implementing and sustaining the proposed grant-funded project.

Outcome objective: An objective that states the results of an activity or the change that occurs in people or the community as a result of the activity taking place. For example, demonstrating that students increased their learning because they received tutoring. Things achieved if we accomplish outcome objectives are called "outcomes."

Outcomes: The changes that take place in an individual, group, or community as a result of grant-funded activities. Differentiated from "outputs," in that outcomes cannot be counted but must be measured.

Outputs: The direct product of grant-funded activities, such as the number of people who received services or the number of an item that was produced. Usually identified by the fact that outputs can be counted.

Pass-through funds: Grant funds that are awarded to an intermediary or pass-through organization that then re-awards those funds to subrecipients.

Pass-through organization: An organization that receives grant funds for the purpose of re-awarding those funds to other organizations, called subrecipients.

Portable Document Format (PDF): An electronic file. Several free readers exist for reading PDF files, including Adobe Acrobat. Grants.gov requires applicants to have the ability to convert documents for submission into PDF format.

Percentage of effort: A method of explaining how much time a person will spend on the grant project. Someone who will work forty hours per week works at 100 percent effort. Someone who contributes five hours per week is giving 12.5 percent effort.

Performance indicator: The criterion on which the success of a project will be measured, e.g., the percentage of change of the number of students enrolled in higher education by the end of the grant period.

Performance target: A specific measure expected to be achieved by the grant-funded program, such as the number or percentage by which the measure will increase or decrease.

Process objective: An objective measuring or counting the outputs of project activities, such as the number of patients screened for cancer or the number of workshops taught.

Project/program: What you are requesting the grant to allow your organization to do. A project may be renovating Section 8 housing, training English as a Second Language teachers, or encouraging people to exercise more.

Project director: The person in charge of running the grant-funded program once it is awarded. May be paid from grant funds or contributed by the applicant organization.

Qualitative data: Data derived from less precise sources, such as staff log notes, questionnaires, and interviews.

Quantitative data: Data derived from objective numerical sources, such as test scores, compilations of survey results, or database reports (such as number served, number who improved performance, etc.).

Quasi-experimental design: Evaluating the effect of the intervention by comparing those served by the project with a group not served by the project.

Request for Application/Request for Proposal (RFA/RFP): See *guidance/guidelines*.

Service area: The geographic area, such as county, state, city, or group of census tracts, that is the focus of your proposed program's services.

SF-424: The grant application cover sheet required of most federal applications. The "SF" stands for "Standard Form." It is usually the first form in an application package.

SMART objectives: Objectives that are specific, measurable, attainable, reasonable, and time limited.

Subawardees/subrecipients: Organizations that receive grant funds from pass-through or intermediary organizations or are partners in projects with other organizations.

Summative evaluation: Assessment of a project's results at the end of the project period or at the end of each year of a multiyear grant for the purpose of determining the project's long-term success and reporting on what was learned by what the project accomplished.

Supplanting: Replacing funds already being spent to conduct an activity with federal funds.

Target population: The people you intend to reach by the grant—sometimes limited by some factor such as age or income level or defined by a segment of the population such as individuals diagnosed with mental illness.

Timeline: A calendar of key grant activities or project milestones that demonstrates that all planned activities can be reasonably accomplished within the proposed project period.

Unallowable costs: Items that the funding agency or cost principles state are not allowed to be purchased or obtained with grant funds. For example, alcohol and fundraising are always unallowable. Whether furniture is unallowable depends on the agency.

Work plan: A table, chart, or narrative description of major grant activities, usually including who is responsible for implementing activities and when the activities will take place. Sometimes also includes proposed evaluative measures or projected outcomes of grant activities. Interchangeable with *action plan*.

Appendix B

Federal Funding Agencies

G rants.gov provides a list of all federal grant-making agencies. They are also listed below, along with a very brief summary of some of the types of grant each agency funds. While we include links to each agency with its listing, we recommend that you supplement your search for funding opportunities through Grants.gov. Not every agency has an easy-to-find grants section on its website, and many list only currently open opportunities. Remember when searching Grants.gov to use the "advanced search" feature so that you may search for archived and closed opportunities instead of only currently open opportunities.

Hint for following links below: All URLs were accurate at the time of publication. Websites are constantly being reorganized. If you find that our link to a page about grants does not work for a particular agency, truncate the link so that you get to the agency's home page (such as epa.gov) and then search within that website for grants information.

Agency for International Development (USAID)

The Agency for International Development is an independent federal government agency that provides economic and humanitarian assistance in more than one hundred countries to ensure a better future for us all.

usaid.gov/work-usaid/get-grant-or-contract

Appalachian Regional Commission (ARC)

The Appalachian Regional Commission is a federal-state partnership that provides grants for community and economic development in the Appalachia region.

www.arc.gov/grants

Christopher Columbus Fellowship Foundation

The Christopher Columbus Fellowship Foundation is an independent federal government agency established to "encourage and support research, study and labor designed to produce new discoveries in all fields of endeavor for the benefit of mankind." It makes "awards" that it characterizes as "competitions," not grants.

columbusfdn.org

Corporation for National and Community Service (CNCS)

The Corporation for National and Community Service is the nation's largest grant maker supporting service and volunteering. Through Senior Corps, AmeriCorps, and Learn and Serve America programs, CNCS is a catalyst for change and offers every American a chance to contribute through service and volunteering.

nationalservice.gov/for_organizations/funding/nofa.asp

Department of Agriculture (USDA)

The Department of Agriculture makes grants in multiple areas, including antihunger, stewardship of national forests and rangelands, product safety, and conservation. The USDA opens markets for American farmers and ranchers and provides food for needy people around the world.

usda.gov

As of publication, this website did not maintain a single list of grants available. Because USDA makes grants through multiple subagencies, it is best to search for "grant" on the site's internal search engine.

Department of Commerce

The Department of Commerce fosters and promotes the nation's economic development and technological advancement through vigilance in international trade policy, domestic business policy and growth, and promoting economic progress at all levels.

commerce.gov/about-commerce/grants-contracting-trade-opportunities

Department of Defense (DOD)

In addition to operating our nation's military forces, the Department of Defense (and its subsidiary departments, such as the Army Corps of Engineers and the Office of Naval Research) makes grants for research in several fields, including aeronautics, communications, psychological and physical health, flood control, and more.

defense.gov

As of publication, we recommend searching for grant opportunities at DOD through Grants.gov.

Department of Education

The Department of Education works to supplement and complement educational efforts on all levels, encouraging increased involvement by the public, parents, and students. Grants are made to support educational programs and research from prekindergarten through graduate-level education.

ed.gov/fund/grants-apply.html

Department of Energy (DOE)

The Department of Energy's goals are to advance national, economic, and energy security in the United States and to promote scientific and technological innovation in support of that goal. Grants are made for programs and research in all aspects of energy production, storage, and transmission, as well as conservation.

energy.gov/public-services/funding-opportunities

Department of Health and Human Services (HHS)

The Department of Health and Human Services contains many subsidiary agencies, such as the Centers for Disease Control and Prevention (CDC) and the Food and Drug Administration (FDA), as well as several others. Grants are made for research and programs in health care, food safety, communicable diseases, and medical education.

hhs.gov/grants

Department of Homeland Security (DHS)

The Department of Homeland Security includes the Federal Emergency Management Agency (FEMA) and the Department of Transportation Security. As such, it has responsibility for research and program grants in a wide array of areas. The most well known include grants for disaster relief to support emergency responders, for protection of mass transit systems, and for national security.

dhs.gov/grant-funding

Department of Housing and Urban Development (HUD)

The Department of Housing and Urban Development makes grants to increase homeownership, support community development, and increase access to affordable housing free from discrimination. HUD publishes a document called the *General Section* that serves as a sort of "master NOFA." It describes the requirements applicable to all of HUD's individual program NOFAs.

portal.hud.gov/hudportal/HUD?src=/program_offices/administration/grants/fundsavail

Department of the Interior (DOI)

The Department of the Interior protects and provides access to the nation's natural and cultural heritage, including responsibilities to Indian tribes and island communities. Some of its subsidiary agencies include the National Park Service, Bureau of Land Management, and Fish and Wildlife Service. The department makes grants for the protection, restoration, and conservation of natural resources for scientific, commercial, and recreational uses, including ecological research.

doi.gov/pmb/partnerships/funding.cfm

Department of Justice (DOJ)

The Department of Justice makes grants related to law enforcement, victims' rights, violence against women, juvenile justice, and sex offenders. Department agencies include the Office on Violence Against Women, Office of Juvenile Justice and Delinquency Prevention, and the Office for Victims of Crime.

justice.gov/business

Department of Labor (DOL)

The Department of Labor makes grants that foster and promote the welfare of job seekers, wage earners, and retirees by improving their working conditions, advancing their opportunities, protecting their retirement and health benefits, and generally protecting worker rights and monitoring national economic measures.

dol.gov/dol/business.htm

Department of State

The Department of State makes grants for US programs and programs to be delivered abroad. Areas of interest include human trafficking, displaced persons/refugees, human rights, and more. Under its Bureau of Educational and Cultural Affairs, the agency makes grants for the international exchange of scholars, students, and administrators and awards individual fellowships, including the Fulbright awards.

state.gov

As of publication, we recommend searching for grants through each of the Department of State's subagencies or by using Grants.gov.

Department of Transportation (DOT)

The Department of Transportation is responsible for all areas of transportation, from the Federal Aviation Administration (FAA) to pedestrian trails and everything in between. Its grant making ranges from energy-efficient and alternative energy public transit projects to streets and bridges in rural areas to increasing safety at rail crossings.

www.dot.gov/grants

Department of the Treasury

The Department of Treasury makes grants to support financial literacy and stability. The types of programs supported include volunteer income tax assistance, assisting low-income taxpayers who have disputes with the IRS, and community development financial institutions.

treasury.gov/services/pages/grants-loans-and-financial-assistance.aspx

Department of Veterans Affairs (VA)

The Department of Veterans Affairs makes grants to organizations providing veterans with a wide range of services. These include patient care, family services, mental health services, sports programs, homeless services, and veterans cemeteries.

va.gov

As of publication, we recommend searching for grants from this agency through Grants.gov.

Environmental Protection Agency (EPA)

The Environmental Protection Agency makes a broad array of grants focused on protecting human health and the environment. Some grants are made to states, tribes, or communities; some to schools or community-based nonprofits; and some to institutions of higher education for student projects.
>   **epa.gov/epahome/grants.htm**

Institute of Museum and Library Services (IMLS)

The Institute of Museum and Library Services is the primary source of federal support for the nation's 122,000 libraries and 17,500 museums. It also funds historical societies, archives, and other organizations that have collections to preserve or display.
>   **imls.gov/applicants/available_grants.aspx**

National Aeronautics and Space Administration (NASA)

As would be expected, the National Aeronautics and Space Administration funds education, programs, and research having to do with STEM education, climate change, and space.
>   **www.nasa.gov**

As of publication, we recommend searching for NASA grants through Grants.gov.

National Archives and Records Administration (NARA)

The National Archives and Records Administration generally makes grants to support scholars who need to access to presidential libraries or NARA for their research. Some funding also goes to support preservation and accessibility of records and archives and publication of papers dependent on sources found in NARA's collections.
>   **archives.gov/grants**

National Endowment for the Arts (NEA)

The National Endowment for the Arts supports excellence in the arts, bringing the arts to all Americans, and arts education. NEA is the largest national source of funds for the arts.
>   **arts.gov/grants**

National Endowment for the Humanities (NEH)

The National Endowment for the Humanities makes grants to support research, education, preservation, and public programs in all aspects of the humanities. Faculty fellowships are also available, as are grants for professional development for teachers.
>   **neh.gov/grants**

National Science Foundation (NSF)

The National Science Foundation promotes the progress of science and funds approximately 20 percent of basic research at colleges and universities. Grants are not limited to research. They are available for an incredible array of program types to a diverse set of eligible recipients.
>   **nsf.gov/funding**

Nuclear Regulatory Commission (NRC)

Although this agency is not primarily a grant-making agency, some US Nuclear Regulatory Commission grants are available for higher education, including curriculum development, faculty development, scholarships, and minority-serving institutions.

nrc.gov/about-nrc/grants.html

Small Business Administration (SBA)

The Small Business Administration's few grants are usually for technical assistance (to offer resources to small-business owners) or education (such as entrepreneurship classes). The agency's own website provides links only to information on research programs, Small Business Innovation Research (SBIR) programs, and Small Business Technology Transfer (STTR) programs. Must search Grants.gov for access to other grant announcements.

sba.gov/category/navigation-structure/loans-grants

Social Security Administration (SSA)

The Social Security Administration, although not primarily a grant-making agency, funds research and demonstration grants that add to existing knowledge and improve methods of managing SSA programs, such as the old-age survivors program, disability insurance, and SSI.

socialsecurity.gov/oag/grants/ssagrant.htm

Appendix C

Registering with Grants.gov and Submitting Proposals

It is important for your organization to begin the process of registering for Grants.gov as soon as you think it is likely that you will be applying for federal grants. This is because the registration is a multistep process, and you may have to rely on others in your organization for completing some of the steps. It takes time.

Fortunately, Grants.gov has available on its website a very useful, step-by-step guide to registration. This free user's guide has screen shots and very clear instructions for each step of the process. You can go to this web address and choose the "Grants.gov Applicant User Guide" from among the links provided on the Applicant Resources page: www.grants.gov/web/grants/applicants/applicant-resources.html

We provide only a brief overview of the process here, but we urge you to rely on the most current version of the user guide available from the Grants.gov website.

Registration Overview

We have reproduced a short flowchart on the next page, courtesy of Grants.gov, to illustrate the steps to complete registration for an organization to submit grants through Grants.gov. These are the steps you should follow.

Notice that the first two steps take place outside the Grants.gov system and require you to confirm or complete registrations with external organizations.

Registration Major Steps

Step One: Obtaining DUNS Number

Every business entity in the United States has a Data Universal Number System (DUNS) number issued by the company Dun & Bradstreet. First, look up your organization's name to

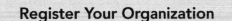

Register Your Organization

Submitting a grant **on behalf of** a company, state, local or tribal government, academia or research institution, not-for-profit or any other institution

---

Step 1: Obtain Data Universal Number (DUNS)

Step 2: Register your organization with the System for Award Management (SAM)

Step 3: Create a username and password

Step 4: Authorize Authorized Organizational Representative (AOR)

Step 5: Track AOR status

Source: Grants.gov User Guide, version December 2012

ensure that a number has not already been assigned (http://fedgov.dnb.com/webform/CCRSearch.do). If one has not, you may request a number online (fedgov.dnb.com/webform/index.jsp). It is best if the chief financial officer or other authorizing official of your organization completes this process. The request can take twenty-four hours to fulfill.

Once your organization has a DUNS number, the number is permanent. No updating or renewals are necessary.

Step Two: Registering with SAM

The System for Award Management (SAM) is a required registry for any vendors doing business with the federal government. This includes organizations receiving grants. SAM replaced previously required registration systems such as the Central Contractor Registry (CCR).

If your organization has applied for federal grants in the past, it has an existing CCR record. The record was migrated to SAM. Similar to searching for an existing DUNS number, you can search the SAM site for your organization's old CCR record (sam.gov). However, your old CCR user name and password will not work with SAM, and you will have to create new ones to access your records.

Note: Grants.gov states that it can take as long as two weeks before a new SAM registration becomes active. You cannot submit a grant proposal until your SAM account is working.

The Grants.gov *Applicant User Guide* will guide you through the SAM registration process if you have to create a new record.

Your registration with SAM must be updated annually.

POCs, MPINs, and AORs

There are some important terms you need to understand so that your Grants.gov and SAM experiences go smoothly. These primarily have to do with the roles of various personnel and the sometimes confusing names given to these roles by the federal system:

◆ *Authorized Organizational Representative (AOR).* An AOR is a person at your organization who is authorized to submit grant applications to Grants.gov. It is better if only the grant professional and one alternate person are granted this role.

◆ *SAM Point of Contact (POC).* This should be the name, phone number, and email address of a person at your organization who is reliable and can be counted on to renew the SAM registration annually.

◆ *E-Business Point of Contact (E-POC).* This is a very important role that you need to pay attention to. The E-POC receives an email from SAM anytime a person requests to be granted AOR status on behalf of your organization, and the E-POC is the only person who can grant this authorization. Since the person designated as the E-POC is often someone in the business office or finance division, removed from daily grants work, that person can forget the E-POC role or not understand the AOR request email when it arrives. We have known grant applications to be delayed because the E-POC just ignored the request to make someone an AOR.

◆ *MPIN.* The MPIN is more of a "what" than a "who." It acts like a PIN number or password in other government systems, so make a note of the MPIN assigned or generated during the SAM registration process.

It is a good idea for the grant professional to keep a record of all the relevant POCs as well as the MPIN in the grants office, as no one else at the organization is likely to have a complete grasp of all these roles or their importance.

Important: If you plan to be one of your organization's AORs and you also wish to serve as the E-Business POC, the system will allow you to do this, but it requires that you register with Grants.gov as an AOR and provide an email address that is different from the email address associated with your E-Business POC account on SAM. Once you register yourself as the AOR, you will have to log in as the E-POC to approve your AOR request.

Step Three: Obtaining a Username and Password for the AOR

Finally, after having completed the required tasks regarding the DUNS number and SAM registration, you are ready to create an account in Grants.gov for yourself to serve as the AOR. Your organization's SAM registration must be complete and activated before you can proceed with this step.

Remember, despite the fact that you will now create an account for yourself or someone else as an individual AOR to use Grants.gov, you are doing so on behalf of an organization. So, you still follow the links and steps for registering an organization, not an individual.

Your AOR account will be linked to your organization's DUNS number. It is possible for a person to serve as AOR for multiple organizations, because each AOR is linked to a DUNS number, not to an individual. You have to create a new Grants.gov account for every AOR role you wish to take on. At this time, Grants.gov is not able to allow individuals who submit grants on behalf of multiple organizations to have more than one DUNS number associated with simply one master AOR account.

In addition, we strongly recommend that you have a second AOR as a backup for your organization, so you can send that person to the registration page to complete his or her own registration as well.

Step Four: AOR Authorization

Remember, once you have requested a username and password to serve as an AOR, the E-Business POC must approve that request before you will have access to Grants.gov. It's a good idea to let the E-POC know to watch for an email and how important it is to respond promptly.

You might also want to provide your E-POC with excerpted pages from the *Applicant User Guide* that uses screen shots to walk the E-POC through the easy process of approving an AOR request.

If the E-POC acts quickly, this step of the process can take less than a few hours to complete.

Step Five: Track AOR Status

To be honest, if everything in the first four steps has gone as planned, you will not have to proceed to step five. But there is a process by which you can log on to Grants.gov and request to see the status of your request to be approved as an AOR.

How the AOR Submits a Grant Application

To submit a grant application through Grants.gov, you must download the application package associated with your grant program from the Grants.gov website. This is not the same thing as downloading the RFA.

Once you have completed the application package and have used the "Check Package for Errors" button, you are ready to follow the process for "Save & Submit." Once you hit "Save & Submit," you will be sent to the "Sign and Submit Application" screen and asked to log in to Grants.gov as the AOR.

Appendix D

Federal Grant Reviewing Opportunities: Selected Links to Federal Agency Sites for Peer Reviewers

Agency for International Development

◆ Higher Education for Development (HED)

HED programs draw volunteers for peer review panels from a pool of scholars at institutions of higher education. To volunteer, contact HED at hedprogram.org.

Corporation for National and Community Service

egrants.cns.gov/espan/main/newaccount.jsp

Department of Agriculture

◆ National Institute of Food and Agriculture
www.csrees.usda.gov/business/prs.html

◆ National Sustainable Agriculture Coalition
sustainableagriculture.net/take-action/advocacy-toolkit/grant-reviewer

Department of Education

It seems as if different directorates within the Department of Education frequently release their own calls for reviewers that are time sensitive to particular competitions. Start with the links below, but also follow pages of any directorates you are interested in.

◆ Office of Elementary and Secondary Education—Race to the Top District
ed.gov/programs/racetothetop-district

◆ Office of Innovation and Improvement
www2.ed.gov/programs/innovation/peerreviewcall.html

◆ Office of Postsecondary Education
   g5.gov or www2.ed.gov/about/offices/list/ope/trio/seekingfieldreaders.html

◆ Office of Special Education and Rehabilitative Services
   www2.ed.gov/about/offices/list/osers/nidrr/nidrrpeerreview.html

Department of Energy

◆ Office of Science
   science.energy.gov/ber/funding-opportunities/peer-review-policy

Department of Health and Human Services

◆ Administration for Children and Families (ACF)
   acfgo.com

◆ Health Resources and Services Administration (HRSA)
   rrm.grantsolutions.gov/AgencyPortal/hrsa.aspx

◆ National Institutes of Health: Center for Scientific Review
   public.csr.nih.gov/pages/default.aspx

◆ Office of Community Services and Office of Public Health and Science
   rrm.grantsolutions.gov

◆ Substance Abuse and Mental Health Services Administration (SAMHSA)
   samhsa.gov/grants/emailform/index.aspx

Department of Homeland Security

◆ Federal Emergency Management Agency

   If you are a member of any of the nine stakeholder organizations (International Association of Fire Chiefs, International Association of Firefighters, National Volunteer Fire Council, National Fire Protection Association, National Association of State Fire Marshals, International Association of Arson Investigators, International Society of Fire Service Instructors, North American Fire Training Directors, or Congressional Fire Services Institute), send your resume and request to be considered a reviewer to your organization. If you are not a member of one of the above organizations, you can try sending an email to any program officer and request that it be forwarded to the appropriate person.

Department of Housing and Urban Development

Apply online through third-party provider, North American Management: namgt.com/gmc.

Department of Justice

- ◆ Office of Justice Programs, Bureau of Justice Assistance
  bja.gov/faqdetail.aspx?id=191

- ◆ Office of Justice Programs

  Send an email to ojppeerreview@lmbps.com.

- ◆ Office of Juvenile Justice and Delinquency Prevention

  Send an email to ojjdpconsultantpool@usdoj.gov.

Department of Labor

doleta.gov/doc/grant_panelist.cfm

Environmental Protection Agency

epa.gov/ncer/peerreview

Institute for Museum and Library Services

imls.gov/reviewers/reviewers.shtm

National Archives and Records Administration

If you wish to be a reviewer for NARA, contact your State Historical Records Agency. Many reviewers are recommended by their state organizations.

National Endowment for the Arts

Contact program officers for information on review panels: arts.gov.

National Endowment for the Humanities

securegrants.neh.gov/prism

National Science Foundation

nsf.gov/bfa/dias/policy/merit_review/reviewer.jsp

Appendix E

Checklist of Organizational Information and Documents for Grant Proposals

- ❑ Organization's full legal name
- ❑ Organization's address, phone, and fax
- ❑ Phone and email of grant contact person
- ❑ Tax ID (EIN) and DUNS numbers
- ❑ IRS 501(c)(3) letter
- ❑ Organization's mission statement
- ❑ Board roster
- ❑ Most current annual budget
- ❑ Most recent audited financials
- ❑ Most recent IRS Form 990
- ❑ Organizational chart
- ❑ Articles of Incorporation
- ❑ Bylaws
- ❑ Resumes of key personnel:
    - ❖ Executive director
    - ❖ Program director/principal investigator
- ❑ Job descriptions for positions to be filled with grant funds
- ❑ Signed certifications and assurances (SF-424B or SF-424D)

Appendix F

How to Select a Grant Consultant

Here are some quick tips about how to find a grant consultant:

◆ Ask colleagues at other organizations in your community for a recommendation.

◆ Check the Grant Professionals Association (GPA) consultant directory. GPA members are required to adhere to a code of ethics (see Appendix M).

◆ Check to see if your community has a local GPA chapter.

◆ Ask if any of your partners in the project have a grant writer who can spearhead the project.

◆ Ask your local United Way for recommendations.

◆ Conduct a web search for "grant consultants."

What to Look for in a Grant Consultant

Of course, you do not have to require that your consultant meet every single one of the qualifications or standards listed here, but they can help you make a good selection:

◆ Years of experience as a grant professional

◆ Experience with and understanding of the purpose and expectations of programs like yours

◆ Experience and success with writing proposals for the particular grant program to which you are applying

◆ Writing samples prepared for previous clients if they are available for review (significant portions may be redacted out of the sample for confidentiality purposes)

◆ Client references that you are allowed to contact

◆ Membership in the Grant Professionals Association or an assurance that the person follows the GPA Code of Ethics

◆ Evidence that the person has earned a credential, such as the Grants Professional Certified (GPC), indicating that an individual has gained a baseline level of knowledge, skills, and experience over a period of years

Appendix G

Federal/State Funding Opportunity Feasibility Analysis

Funding opportunity name: _____ Today's date: _____

Deadline: _____ Size of awards: _____ per year for _____ years

Match required? ❏ Yes ❏ No   If yes, at what ratio? _____

Total number of pages to be submitted: _____

Prioritized Checklist for Reviewing an RFA

Category	Assessment Question	Yes	No
Purpose	Is there a close match between our organization's mission and experience and the funding agency's purpose for providing this grant?		
Eligibility	Is our type of organization eligible for this opportunity?		
Deadline	Is the time between now and the deadline sufficient for us to prepare this proposal?		
Funding amount	Can we fit the budget for our proposed program between the funding floor (minimum grant allowed) and the funding ceiling (maximum award)?		
Matching requirements	Can we meet any matching funds requirement?		
Type of match required	May in-kind contributions count toward the match?		
Number of awards	Is the number of anticipated awards high enough that our organization is likely to be competitive?		
Partnering requirements	Do we have time to establish relationships, or do we have existing relationships with required partners, or are we members of an eligible coalition?		
Level of evaluation	Do we have the resources and expertise (and are there sufficient funds allowed in the grant budget) to hire an external evaluator or for us to complete the level of evaluation expected by this agency?		
Regularity of competition	Will we have another opportunity to apply for this program in the future if we decide not to pursue it now?		
Technical assistance	Will there be a workshop or webinar offered by the funding agency to help applicants know how to apply?		
Prior experience	Will new applicants receive as many points as applicants with previous grants or prior experience?		
Priority/bonus points	Can we meet any required or optional competitive preference priorities or otherwise earn bonus points?		

Decision to write this proposal: ❏ Yes ❏ No   Approved by: _____

Appendix H

Budget Planning Checklist (adapted from the University of Georgia)

PERSONNEL
- [ ] Position or Name
- [ ] % Time / effort on project
- [ ] Length of time expected to work
- [ ] What will they be doing?

   * Do NOT list consultants here; they go under Contractual

FRINGE BENEFITS
- [ ] Total allowable fringe benefits

   Provide calculation %.

TRAVEL
- [ ] Purpose of trip
- [ ] Destination (if known).
- [ ] Number of travelers
- [ ] Estimated Cost per trip/person (include airfare, mileage, parking, tolls, public transportation, meals, and lodging; or use federal per diem tables)
- [ ] Conference fees

   *International Travel is usually NOT ALLOWED

PUBLICATION CHARGES
- [ ] Commercial printing or publication charges for brochures, program materials, stationery, etc.

EQUIPMENT
Equipment greater than or equal to $5,000 and has a useful life of more than 1 year.
- [ ] Type / description
- [ ] Estimated Cost
- [ ] Narrative on intended use in project.

   * Permanent capital expenditures (e.g. land, buildings, etc) are usually NOT ALLOWED; check funder guidelines

UTILITIES/FACILITIES CHARGES
- [ ] Meeting, classroom, or program space.
- [ ] Long distance, Internet access, directly attributable utilities such as electricity, etc.

COST SHARING / MATCHING FUNDS
- [ ] Matching funds/cost share required
  ___ to 1 match (such as 1 to 1, 2 to 1, etc.)
- [ ] Total amount of cash and non-cash cost sharing that is available to the project
- [ ] Matching funds and value of in-kind contributions should be shown in the Organization column
- [ ] Budget justification clearly identifies cash and in-kind contributions.

MATERIALS & SUPPLIES
Purchases under $5,000 are considered supplies, even computers.
- [ ] Typical operating supplies: office supplies, software, education or field supplies.
- [ ] Office "equipment": computers, printers, projectors.
- [ ] Non-typical supplies – submitted with brief narrative and estimated cost breakdown.

CONSULTING / CONTRACTUAL AGREEMENTS
- [ ] Consultant to be Used
- [ ] Services to be Provided
- [ ] Basis for Cost Estimate
- [ ] Deliverables
- [ ] Letter of Agreement or Contract on file

ALL OTHER DIRECT COSTS
- [ ] Direct project charges not included in other categories. Description and cost must be included in budget narrative for each item.
- [ ] Other / Miscellaneous all must be detailed and identified.

Some examples of direct charges include:

Communications – mailings, postage, faxes, telephone

Photocopying – in-house copying (not commercial printing) for materials associated to the program.

Service Maintenance – Maintenance contracts in direct correlation to use of equipment for the project (e.g. 50% use of equipment for project, 50% of service contract applied to budget costs).

Conference / Meetings – includes costs of holding a conference or meeting. (e.g. Rental of facilities, equipment for meeting, honorariums, speaker fees, travel and per Diems for participants.) Provide detail in the budget narrative.

Speaker / Trainer Fees – Provide speaker information, description of services and fee.

Honorariums – Provide recipient information (if known) or number expected, reason for need, and fee associated with the honorarium.

Subcontracts – Include a plan of work, budget, and detailed budget narrative. Use these same required budgetary detail guidelines.

Consultants – Provide the name & organization of the consultant, a statement of work, a breakdown of funds being charged to the project. (e.g. number of days of service, rate of pay, travel per Diem, etc.) Also provide a copy of the resume or vita.

INDIRECT COSTS
- [ ] If indirect costs are allowed by funder. Provide negotiated rate or required %.

Appendix I

Selected List of Data Sources

Federal Government Sources (in alphabetical order)

Administration for Children and Families—acf.hhs.gov

Provides data regarding issues impacting children and families, but requires some searching.

Agency for Healthcare Research and Quality—ahrq.gov

Provides information on health care issues and trends as well as evidenced-based practices.

Bureau of Labor statistics—bls.gov

Provides information on unemployment rates, average hourly earnings, costs of benefits, and more.

Census—census.gov

You can easily click on a quick snapshot of data at the national, state, county, and city levels. With a little practice, you can break it down into even smaller chunks, such as tracts and block groups, to get at data that is very specific to a particular locality. Also accessed at the Census site, American Community Survey data produces estimates for numerous social, economic, and housing characteristics, including language, education, the commute to work, employment, mortgage status, and rent, as well as income, poverty, veteran status, and health insurance.

Centers for Disease Control—cdc.gov

Great information on a variety of health issues ranging from Alzheimer's disease to obesity to infectious diseases and bioterrorism.

Child Welfare Information Gateway—childwelfare.gov

Information regarding child welfare issues, strengthening families, child abuse and neglect, foster care, and adoption. Bonus: a logic model builder.

Department of Labor—dol.gov

And its Employment and Training Division—doleta.gov

Useful for workforce development and education grants to project job growth by industry, how much workers earn in various positions, and what skills and education people need to enter those jobs.

National Center for Educational Statistics—nces.ed.gov

The website provides information about school districts, private school information, information about higher education, and trend information.

National Center for Science and Engineering Statistics—nsf.gov/statistics

Provides statistical data on the US science and engineering enterprise, including research and development, the science and engineering workforce, the condition and progress of STEM education, and US competitiveness in science, engineering, technology, and R&D.

Office of Rural Health Policy—hrsa.gov/ruralhealth

Has good information on rural health issues and statistics that will help draw immediate attention to issues.

Office of Women's Health—womenshealth.gov

Publishes two data books: (1) *Women's Health USA*, which highlights emerging issues and trends in women's health, and (2) *Women's Health Profiles by State*.

Substance Abuse and Mental Health Services Administration—SAMHSA.gov

Maintains the Drug Abuse Warning Network (DAWN), the Drug and Alcohol Services Information System (DASIS), the National Mental Health Reporting Program, and the National Survey on Drug Use and Health (NSDUH), as well as good information on evidenced-based practices.

Private Sources of National Data

Annie E. Casey Foundation Kids Count Reports—kidscount.org

Publishes data focused on the well-being of children for all fifty states, Washington, DC, Puerto Rico, and the US Virgin Islands.

Pew Research Center—pewresearch.org

Describes itself as a "nonpartisan fact tank." Pew tracks issues, attitudes, and trends. It operates multiple projects, including the Research Center for People & the Press, Project for

Excellence in Journalism, Internet and American Life Project, Forum on Religion and Public Life, the Hispanic Center, the Global Attitudes Project, and the Social and Demographic Trends project. The Social & Demographic Trends section and the Pew Hispanic Center are discussed below.

Pew Center's on Social and Demographic Trends

Excellent reports on generational issues, race and gender issues, and economic issues.

Pew Hispanic Center

"Seeks to improve understanding of the US Hispanic population and chronicle Latino's growing impact on the nation." Good resource for a variety of matters regarding Hispanics/Latinos, including demographics, economics and personal finance, education, identity (specifically opinions on race), and language use.

The Association of Religion Data Archives—thearda.com

Religion statistics, denominational profiles, maps, and reports that provide information on religious affiliation, as well as a GIS tool that can be helpful in community asset mapping.

Appendix J

Tips for Hiring an External Evaluator

Here are some quick tips about how to find an evaluator who is a good match for your program:

◆ Ask previous grantees in this program to recommend an evaluator.

◆ Agree to an "evaluation swap" in which the project director of your program evaluates another program and that program's director evaluates your program.

◆ Ask your local United Way for recommendations.

◆ Ask the program officer if the funding agency is able to recommend someone.

◆ Inquire at the local university's research office.

◆ Inquire among university faculty doing work in the field of your project.

◆ Search at the American Evaluation Association (eval.org), whose members are required to adhere to a code of ethics.

◆ Conduct a web search for "evaluation firm."

Qualifications to Look for in an Evaluator

Of course, you do not have to require every evaluator to meet every one of these qualifications, but they can be a good guideline when making your selection:

◆ Years of experience evaluating federal/state programs

◆ Experience with and understanding of the purpose and expectations of programs like yours

◆ Copies of evaluation reports prepared for previous clients if they are available for review (sometimes evaluators consider these confidential or must redact out the names of clients before they can share samples with you)

◆ Client references that you are allowed to contact

◆ Membership in the American Evaluation Association or an assurance that the person follows the AEA Code of Ethics

Appendix K

List of Websites Mentioned by Chapter

Chapter One

Federal Register—daily publication that lists rules, public notices, and requests for proposals from all federal agencies
  federalregister.gov

Grants.gov—federal website for searching grant opportunities, downloading application packages, and submitting grants
  Grants.gov

Chapter Two

White House Office of Faith-based and Neighborhood Partnerships
  whitehouse.gov/administration/eop/ofbnp

System for Award Management (SAM)
  sam.gov

Chapter Three

Puget Sound Grantwriters Association article on how to hire a grant consultant
  grantwriters.org/how-to-hire-a-freelancer

Chapter Four

Catalog of Federal Domestic Assistance (CFDA)—describes more than 2,200 federal assistance programs
  cfda.gov

Chapter Six

Kellogg Foundation Free Guide to Developing Logic Models
  wkkf.org/knowledge-center/resources/2006/02/wk-kellogg-foundation-logic-model-
  development-guide.aspx

Chapter Seven

Federal per diem tables—site to determine federally allowed rates for lodging, meals, and incidentals in all US major cities and a "general" figure to be used for locations not specifically listed
  gsa.gov/perdiem

COFAR—to learn about the new Uniform Cost Principles and access training videos
  cfo.gov/cofar

Independent Sector—to obtain the dollar value of a volunteer's time
  independentsector.org/volunteer_time

IRS rates for mileage—to search for mileage rates for the current year
  irs.gov

Introduction to Indirect Costs for grant professionals
  grantsnorthwest.com/indirect-costs-in-federal-grants

Chapter Nine

US Census Bureau—for obtaining a wide range of data about particular geographic areas
  census.gov

Chapter Thirteen

American Evaluation Association—suggested site to find an external evaluator for your program. Members are required to adhere to a code of ethics
  eval.org

Edna McConnell Clark Foundation—a summary of the foundation's four categories of evaluation measures
  emcf.org

Appendix L

Recommended Reading, Additional Resources, and Training Opportunities

A short list of further reading and professional development opportunities that are resources that one or both of the authors have found to be useful to them in their grant seeking. Neither is meant to be a comprehensive bibliography of all possible books or conferences on a subject.

Books

Beyond the plethora of books on general grant writing that you may find through your library or favorite bookseller, we draw these few titles to your attention as relevant to a particular aspect of federal grant seeking.

Organizational Capacity and Readiness to Submit Proposals

Brophy, Sarah S. *Are You Grant Ready?* Altamira Press, 2005.

Brothers, John and Sherman, Anne. *Building Nonprofit Capacity: A Guide to Managing Change Through Organizational Lifecycles.* Jossey-Bass, 2012.

Drucker, Peter F; (With Jim Collins, et al.) *The Five Most Important Questions You Will Ever Ask About Your Organization.* Leader to Leader Institute, 2008.

Nonprofit Financial Issues

Wells, Michael K., *Grantwriting Beyond the Basics, Book 2, Understanding Nonprofit Finances.* Continuing Education Press, Portland State University, 2006.

Post-Award Management

Margolin, Judith, ed. *After the Grant: The Nonprofit's Guide to Good Stewardship.* The Foundation Center, 2010.

Program Evaluation

Fitzpatrick, Jody L., James R. Sanders and Blaine R. Worthen, *Program Evaluation: Alternative Approaches and Practical Guidelines* (4th Edition). Pearson, 2010.

Grinnell, Robert, Peter A. Gabor, Yvonne A. Unrau, *Program Evaluation for Social Workers* (6th edition). Oxford University Press, 2012.

Mertens, Donna M. and Amy T. Wilson, *Program Evaluation Theory and Practice: A Comprehensive Guide.* Guilford Press, 2012.

Rossi, Peter H., Mark W. Lipsey and Howard E. Freeman, *Evaluation: A Systemic Approach* (7th edition). SAGE Publications, 2003.

Royse, David, Bruce A. Thyer and Deborah K. Padgett, *Program Evaluation: An Introduction* (5th edition). Cengage Learning, 2009.

Websites with Additional Information on Topics from This Book

Federal Cost Principals

Uniform Administrative Requirements, Cost Principles, and Audit Requirements for Federal Awards

federalregister.gov/articles/2013/12/26/2013-30465/uniform-administrative-requirements-cost-principles-and-audit-requirements-for-federal-awards

Indirect Costs

The Grantsmanship Center's guide to understanding indirect costs.
  tgci.com/sites/default/files/pdf/Understanding%20Indirect%20Costs_1.pdf

Understanding indirect costs—Grants Northwest
  grantsnorthwest.com/indirect-costs-in-federal-grants

Logic Models

Innovation Network FREE Online Logic Model Builder
  innonet.org

The World Bank's Logframe Handbook (logframes is their term for logic models)
  www.wau.boku.ac.at/fileadmin/_/H81/H811/Skripten/811332/811332_G3_log-framehandbook.pdf

Professional Development Opportunities

Allow us to introduce you to a few resources that you may use to further develop your skills in a particular area around federal grants. Accessing the website or attending the conference of any of these organizations will immediately introduce you to multiple other resources.

Grant Seeking in General

The Grant Professionals Association (GPA)—GPA is a membership organization for grant professionals responsible for winning proposals for their organizations. The membership serves organizations large and small in private and government grant seeking. Local chapters, a national conference, regional conferences, a journal, and other resources are available.

   grantprofessionals.org

Grant Seeking for Faculty in Higher Education

A relatively new organization, the National Organization of Research Development Professionals supports faculty and institutional research development personnel in securing research funding. The organization develops and shares best practices for attracting and managing research funding.

   nordp.org

Postaward Management

The National Grants Management Association (NGMA)—NGMA is a membership organization for personnel responsible for managing and reporting upon grants after they are funded. The organization provides comprehensive full life-cycle grants management training, professional certification, a national conference, a journal, and other resources.

   www.ngma.org

The National Council of University Research Administrators (NCURA)—NCURA serves those responsible for managing and reporting upon grants after they are funded, primarily in higher-education settings. The organization offers an overall national conference as well as conferences targeting financial managers and preaward personnel (grant writers). Regional meetings, a magazine, and a journal complement the resources available to members.

   ncura.edu

Project Evaluation

The American Evaluation Association (AEA)—The American Evaluation Association is an international professional association of evaluators devoted to all forms of evaluation. AEA offers a national conference, a consultant's directory, a journal, other publications, and an online discussion group. AEA has approximately 7,700 members from all fifty states and more than sixty foreign countries.

   eval.org

Appendix M

Grant Professionals Association Code of Ethics

The Grant Professionals Association is a professional membership organization that builds and supports an international community of grant professionals committed to serving the greater public good by practicing the highest ethical and professional standards.

Revised 10/5/11

The Grant Professionals Association (GPA), a nonprofit membership association, is committed to serving the greater public good by practicing the highest ethical and professional standards. Ethics refer to the rules or standards governing the conduct of a person or members of a profession[1].

Members have joined forces to be the leading authority and resource for the practice of grantsmanship in all sectors of the field. Membership in this association promotes positive relationships between grant professionals and their stakeholders, provides a vehicle for grant professionals to gain professional growth and development, and enhances the public image and recognition of the profession within the greater philanthropic, public, and private funding communities. Members' foundation is stimulated by the rich diversity within the grant profession.

Members, among others, are to:

- Practice their profession with the highest sense of integrity, honesty, and truthfulness to maintain and broaden public confidence

- Adhere to all applicable laws and regulations in all aspects of grantsmanship

- Continually improve their professional knowledge and skills

- Promote positive relationships between grant professionals and their stakeholders

- Value the privacy, freedom, choice and interests of all those affected by their actions

- Ensure that funds are solicited according to program guidelines

- Adhere to acceptable means of compensation for services performed; pro bono work is encouraged

- Foster cultural diversity and pluralistic values and treat all people with dignity and respect

- Become leaders and role models in the field of grantsmanship

- Encourage colleagues to embrace and practice GPA's Code of Ethics and Standards of Professional Practice.

Standards of Professional Practice

As members respect and honor the above principles and guidelines established by the GPA Code of Ethics, any infringement or breach of standards outlined in the Code are subject to disciplinary sanctions, including expulsion, to be determined by a committee elected by their peers.

Professional Obligations:

1. Members shall act according to the highest ethical standards of their institution, profession, and conscience.

2. Members shall obey all applicable local, state, provincial, and federal civil and criminal laws and regulations.

3. Members shall avoid the appearance of any criminal offense or professional misconduct.

4. Members shall disclose all relationships that might constitute, or appear to constitute, conflicts of interest.

5. Members shall not be associated directly or indirectly with any service, product, individuals, or organizations in a way that they know is misleading.

6. Members shall not abuse any relationship with a donor, prospect, volunteer or employee to the benefit of the member or the member's organization.

7. Members shall recognize their individual boundaries of competence and are forthcoming and truthful about their professional experience, knowledge and expertise.

8. Members shall continually strive to improve their personal competence.

Solicitation and Use of Funds:

9. Members shall take care to ensure that all solicitation materials are accurate and correctly reflect the organization's mission and use of solicited funds.

10. Members shall take care to ensure that grants are used in accordance with the grant's intent.

If Applicable:

11. Members shall take care to ensure proper use of funds, including timely reports on the use and management of such funds.

12. Members shall obtain explicit consent by the grantor before altering the conditions of grant agreements.

Presentation of Information:

13. Members shall not disclose privileged information to unauthorized parties. Information acquired from consumers is confidential. This includes verbal and written disclosures, records, and video or audio recording of an activity or presentation without appropriate releases.

14. Members shall not plagiarize[2] in any professional work, including, but not limited to: grant proposals, journal articles/magazines, scholarly works, advertising/marketing materials, websites, scientific articles, self-plagiarism, etc.

15. Members are responsible for knowing the confidentiality regulations within their jurisdiction.

16. Members shall use accurate and consistent accounting methods that conform to the appropriate guidelines adopted by the American Institute of Certified Public Accountants (AICPA) for the type of organization involved. (In countries outside of the United States, comparable authority should be utilized).

Compensation:

17. Members shall work for a salary or fee.

18. Members may accept performance-based compensation, such as bonuses, provided such bonuses are in accordance with prevailing practices within the members' own organizations and are not based on a percentage of grant monies.

19. Members shall not accept or pay a finder's fee,[3] commission,[4] or percentage compensation based on grants and shall take care to discourage their organizations from making such payments.

20. Compensation should not be written into grants unless allowed by the funder.

[1]*Defined by American Heritage Dictionary*

[2]*Plagiarize—to steal or pass off (the ideas or words of another) as one's own; use (another's production) without crediting the source; to commit literary theft; present as new and original an idea or product derived from an existing source.*

[3]*Finder's fee—payment made for introducing a nonprofit to a funder and/or contingent upon the nonprofit receiving a grant from that funder.*

[4]*Commission—flat-rate fee or percentage paid for services rendered when a grant is awarded.*

Index

If you enjoyed this book, you'll want to pick up the other books in the CharityChannel Press **In the Trenches™** series.

CharityChannel.com/bookstore

*Charity*Channel
P R E S S™

And now introducing **For the GENIUS® Press,** an imprint that produces books on just about any topic that people want to learn. You don't have to be a genius to read a GENIUS book, but you'll sure be smarter once you do!

ForTheGENIUS.com/bookstore

61603449R00135

Made in the USA
Middletown, DE
12 January 2018